from
GOSPEL To SERMON
PREACHING SYNOPTIC TEXTS

from GOSPEL TO SERMON
PREACHING SYNOPTIC TEXTS

DAVID J. OURISMAN

Chalice Press

St. Louis, Missouri

Bible quotations, unless otherwise noted, are from the *New Revised Standard Version Bible,* copyright 1989, Division of Christian Education of the National Council of Churches of Christ in the United States of America. Used by permission. All rights reserved.

Those quotations marked RSV are from the *Revised Standard Version of the Bible,* copyright 1952 [2nd edition, 1971] by the Division of Christian Education of the National Council of the Churches of Christ in the United States of America. Used by permission. All rights reserved.

Cover art: Early Christian fresco painting,
        ca. 350 A.D., Catacomb of St. Domitilla, Rome
        Photograph courtesy of Ken Lawrence
Cover design: Michael Domínguez
Art direction: Michael Domínguez
Interior design: Wynn Younker

This book is printed on acid-free, recycled paper.

Visit Chalice Press on the World Wide Web at
www.chalicepress.com

10 9 8 7 6 5 4 3 2 1   00 01 02 03 04

Library of Congress Cataloging–in–Publication Data

Ourisman, David J.
    From Gospel to sermon: preaching synoptic texts / David J. Ourisman.
        p.   cm.
Includes bibliographical references and index.
ISBN 0-8272-1026-4
1. Bible. N.T. Gospels—Homiletical use.   I. Title.
    BS2555.4 .O86   1999
    251—dc21   99-050406

Printed in the United States of America

Contents

99335

To Carol

cousin,
confidante,
and colleague

Acknowledgments

A book, like a sermon, is a journey. Although I cannot possibly mention all those who played roles along the way, I would like to acknowledge those who have made a major contribution to this work. First, the members of my dissertation committee at the Graduate Theological Union helped me develop the basic direction of this research. Mary Donovan Turner was my advisor throughout my doctoral program and the chair of my committee. For her interest and investment in this project since we first spoke of it in 1992, I want to express my gratitude. Joel Green and Daryl Schmidt, from the perspective of New Testament scholarship, and Nancy Burroughs, from the perspective of persuasion theory, have all been quite helpful to me in thinking both about biblical narrative and about preaching.

I have been blessed with many teachers, both within academic settings and beyond. Gordon Winsor of Centre College introduced me to the synoptic gospels, in general, and to Peter's confession, in particular. Donald Juel of Princeton Theological Seminary first piqued my imagination with the possibilities of literary approaches to the gospels. I would be remiss, however, if I failed to mention my most important teachers. The members of the congregations I served for sixteen years—the South Seaville Circuit in Cape May County, New Jersey, and the Monmouth Grace United Methodist Church in Eatontown, New Jersey—have made a profound contribution to my formation as a preacher. The members of Epworth United

Methodist Church in Berkeley, California, have allowed me to test my emerging ideas on them. Finally, my students at Pacific School of Religion and Vancouver School of Theology have actually experimented with my method, and their experiments have helped shape this work in important ways.

I cannot overstate how deeply I value the support and encouragement of my family: my children, Joshua and Jessica, my parents, my sister and my brothers and their families. The greatest surprise of this journey, when I moved to Berkeley and began my work at the GTU, was the discovery of my heretofore unknown cousin, Carol Barriger. At that time she was an M.Div. student at Pacific School of Religion. She is now an ordained minister in the United Church of Christ. Our weekly chats over coffee and tea while attending school together, and our continuing weekly lunches up and down Solano Avenue, have provided much-needed grist, and unfailing enthusiasm, for this book.

Finally, I thank Jon Berquist, my editor at Chalice Press, for his interest in this project and for invaluable advice in helping this book take shape.

1

Tell Me the Stories of Jesus

The Weekly Dilemma

It is Monday morning…again. You are sitting in your study, the lectionary texts for next Sunday open before you, staring you in the face: Proverbs 1:20–33…James 3:1–12…Mark 8:27–38.

Which one do you choose? You have always been drawn to narrative texts; they are so much easier to preach. You begin to look more closely at the lesson from Mark. You read the passage silently, then gaze out the window at the church lawn while you brood. Nothing happens. You read the words out loud. Still, nothing grabs you. It sounds so familiar. Where in the story is something to preach about this week? You sit with your question for a few minutes, then walk down to the kitchen to heat some water for tea, hoping for inspiration to come.

Nearly fifty times a year, as many as two thousand times in the course of our ministry, we preachers find ourselves staring at a biblical text with next Sunday's deadline looming. With the open Bible in front of us and a blank sheet of paper on the desk (or a new document open in the word processor), we find ourselves in search of a message. *How am I to speak a fresh word from this text?* The weekly search for an original insight, for a new angle, for an intriguing

1

perspective, for a creative and effective way to proclaim the word, is both a significant responsibility and a daunting challenge.

As if the sheer number of occasions on which the preacher is called "to get up a sermon," as Fred Craddock put it, were not intimidating enough, consider that the same texts keep coming up again and again. While the Revised Common Lectionary offers the preacher significant benefits, it also means that the preacher will face the identical set of texts every third year. The memories of sermons past, or perhaps just the ingrained patterns of our interpretive style, seem to lead us down the same habitual journeys from text to sermon (just as our sermons tend to picture Jesus walking barefoot down the same dusty paths week after week). Can we preachers open our ears so that we can hear what the readings for the seventeenth Sunday after Pentecost in year B have to say to us *this* year that they have not already said three, six, or nine years ago?

> Twenty minutes later, you are back in your study. The caffeine has kicked in, and you have a new burst of energy. Peter's confession. What can I say about it this year? Your eyes pause briefly on the quarterly journal of preachers' helps lying unopened on the corner of your desk, but you resist the temptation. Though it's written by professional biblical scholars, you've never found it greatly helpful. When you begin with your own hunches about a text, it always seems to lead to a better sermon.
>
> Something occurs to you. You look through the files of last year's sermons, and sure enough, there it is. The end of last August, less than eleven months ago, you preached on the same story. "Child of the Living God, Child of Jonah" you called your sermon. You look back at the text from Mark and notice something about verse 29:
>
>> He asked them, "But who do you say that I am?"
>> Peter answered him, "You are the Messiah."[1]
>
> The phrases you based your whole sermon on last year aren't even in Mark. Peter doesn't call Jesus "Son of the living God," and neither does Jesus call Peter "son of Jonah." As you look more closely, you see a number of other differences as well.

---

[1]All biblical citations are from the *New Revised Standard Version Bible* unless otherwise noted. Translations in the sermons are the author's.

But can this kind of pondering lead to a sermon? You are looking at something that is in the text...or, rather, not in the text...but will it preach? You can imagine exactly which members of the congregation would fold their arms and lean back in the pews...

This is part of the dilemma when we preach from the gospel lesson for the day. We have all noticed how some stories keep appearing. Any number of stories are assigned two out of three years, some every year. How do we preach from different versions of the same "stories"? Do we preach essentially the same sermon, making sure we keep the details right depending on which text we are preaching from? Or are there other possibilities?

Some would argue that it doesn't really matter. Some read the gospels as simply a historical record of the life and teachings of Jesus of Nazareth. From this perspective, Matthew, Mark, Luke, and John are windows into past events. We read them to learn *what really happened*, to hear the things that Jesus said and see the things he did. According to Mark, Peter said to Jesus, "You are the Messiah." Matthew corroborates Mark and adds an additional detail that we would not otherwise know. Peter goes on to say, "the Son of the living God." From this perspective, differences between or among the gospels are not significant for the preacher.

Other readers are not so sure. They wonder if there is not something interesting and worthwhile to be found in the very diversity of the gospels. Redaction criticism is one approach to this question. Redaction critics study the ways in which Matthew, Mark, and Luke have edited the traditional material that has come to them. Paying attention to the differences among versions of a pericope can yield insight into the theological agendas of the authors, but is there more to be discovered? Can we gain a full understanding of Mark's message by focusing only on those places where Mark differs from Matthew and Luke?[2]

As you keep reading the text, you begin to see other ways that the Marcan confession is different from the version you preached on last year. In Matthew's version, Peter receives high praise indeed.

---

[2]Donald H. Juel made this argument in his dissertation, *Messiah and Temple: The Trial of Jesus in the Gospel of Mark,* SBLDS 31 (Missoula, Mont.: Scholars Press, 1977), 43, and again in *A Master of Surprise: Mark Interpreted* (Minneapolis: Fortress Press, 1994), 22.

Blessed are you, Simon son of Jonah! For flesh and blood
has not revealed this to you, but my Father in heaven. And
I tell you, you are Peter, and on this rock I will build my
church, and the gates of Hades will not prevail against it.
I will give you the keys of the kingdom of heaven, and
whatever you bind on earth will be bound in heaven,
and whatever you loose on earth will be loosed in heaven.
(Mt. 16:17–19)

But in Mark, Peter receives none of these compliments. He answers Jesus, "You are the Messiah." The only response Jesus makes
is to "sternly order" the disciples "not to tell anyone about him."
No praise, no recognition of divine inspiration, no conferral of a
new name, no granting of leadership within the church, not even
a hint that Peter answered the question correctly!

You leaf backward and forward through Mark and think about
the picture of the disciples that Mark is painting. It's not so com-
plimentary. They seem so obtuse, so slow to learn, so quick to say
something totally inappropriate. In the end, all of the twelve fail
Jesus: Judas betrays him, Peter denies him, the other ten flee from
him when he is arrested. None of the twelve encounters the risen
Christ or receives a great commission at the end of Mark as they
do at the end of Matthew.

You see that Mark's account of Peter's confession is different
from Matthew's, but you are beginning to see that their stories-
as-a-whole are different as well. Is the way Mark narrates Peter's
confession somehow related to the way he tells the whole story?
Is the meaning of the part somehow tied up in the meaning of
the whole? Is there a sermon *here*?

By asking questions like these, preachers are moving beyond
reading the gospels as history and are beginning to read the gospels
as works of narrative literature. While continuing to affirm that God
has worked through the historical events described by the biblical
narratives, I also want to affirm the importance of the narratives
themselves. By the *way* they tell us the story, the evangelists are making their witness to the church about the meaning of Jesus' life,
death, and resurrection.

What Do We Mean by the "Stories of Jesus"?

The title of this chapter is taken from the gospel song "Tell Me the Stories of Jesus" written by William H. Parker in 1885.

Tell me the stories of Jesus I love to hear;
things I would ask him to tell me if he were here:
scenes by the wayside, tales of the sea,
stories of Jesus, tell them to me.[3]

This phrase can be taken in two very different ways. The more obvious way is to think of the "stories of Jesus" as the individual episodes that took place during Jesus' career, the events to which the four gospels witness: Peter's confession, feeding the five thousand, welcoming the children, calming the storm at sea, and so on. This is surely what William Parker had in mind when he wrote the hymn. The gospels contain dozens of stories when we think of them this way… "scenes by the wayside, tales of the sea."

But what if we think of the "stories of Jesus" in another sense? Whatever else they may be, each of the four gospels—Matthew, Mark, Luke, and John—is a story about Jesus. Or to put it more precisely, each is a *telling* of the same story. We might even think of them as four sermons preached on the same text. Each gospel writer has proclaimed the story of Jesus in a particular way. They begin at different places, end in different ways, and portray the various characters differently. Each conveys a particular theological understanding of the meaning of Jesus' life, death, and resurrection. Each addresses a particular audience: a church in its own situation facing unique challenges and opportunities. Each appropriates the story of Jesus for a particular purpose, whether it be to guide, to challenge, to comfort, to exhort, or to reassure the church. Toward that end, each emphasizes some things and glosses over others, includes some incidents and leaves out others, places greater stress on some details and less on others. These four tellings of the story of Jesus show that the four evangelists had diverse talents in the art of preaching, a differing way with words, peculiar patterns of speaking and writing, and unique gifts of storytelling.

---

[3]William H. Parker, "Tell Me the Stories of Jesus," *Chalice Hymnal* (St. Louis: Chalice Press, 1995), no. 190.

What are the "stories of Jesus" that we preach? Are they self-contained episodes, each with its own message? Or are they stories-as-a-whole that convey the faith and understanding of each of the evangelists? I am encouraging preachers to think of each gospel as a story-of-the-whole. The shift that I am proposing offers new possibilities to preachers seeking a fresh look at overly familiar texts.

When we treat gospel lessons as self-contained stories of Jesus, each one in effect becomes a parable with its own message to preach, its own point to make, its own lesson to teach.[4] After a lifetime of hearing these stories in Sunday school, children's sermons, and church services, and then years of preaching these same stories over and over, we lose the capacity to be surprised by them. Traditional interpretations of those stories ring so loudly in our ears that we cannot hear a new word. They ought to excite the spirit and stir the imagination, but our hearts feel strangely unwarmed.

I am convinced that the new narrative critical studies of the gospels, one of the creative edges of recent biblical scholarship, offer immense promise for preachers. I am calling on preachers to think of the "stories of Jesus" as the four stories-as-a-whole told by Matthew, Mark, Luke, and John. I am urging preachers to read lectionary texts not as isolated stories but as integral parts of the fabric of a larger narrative. I am arguing that the meaning of those isolated stories unfolds when read in the context of the narrative-as-a-whole. There is untapped promise in pursuing such an approach. By inviting the gospels to speak to us as whole narratives, we can move beyond habitual readings of all-too-familiar stories, allowing the gospels to surprise us with insight we did not expect.

Nineteen centuries before the contemporary turn to narrative preaching, Matthew, Mark, Luke, and John were preaching the good news through the medium of narrative. (Paul was also preaching the good news, but he used the medium of logical discourse rather than story.) The evangelists were narrative preachers. Like all storytellers, they conveyed their understanding of the story—their sense of its meaning—by the *way* they told it, by the way they added or left out details, by the way they described its various characters. When we

---

[4]This is the critique of much narrative preaching offered by Charles L. Campbell in *Preaching Jesus: New Directions for Homiletics in Hans Frei's Postliberal Theology* (Grand Rapids, Mich.: Eerdmans, 1997).

listen to Garrison Keillor's stories of Lake Wobegon, we notice how much of the storyteller's point of view is communicated to the listener by the simplest things: a subtle inflection in his tone of voice, a well-chosen detail added to the narration at just the right moment. I am suggesting that the four evangelists were already doing in their first-century contexts what preachers and storytellers are doing today.

Reading and Preaching the Stories of Jesus

What follows is a "how-to" description of *one way* to preach from a sermon text in light of the story-as-a-whole of the synoptic gospel in which that text is found. I have developed this method both through academic study and through experimenting in the local church with different ways of preaching on texts from the synoptics. This chapter will describe the method, and the following chapters will demonstrate its use in developing sermons on Peter's confession in each of the three synoptic gospels.

In Advance of the Lectionary Year

A first reading of the narrative. I am encouraging preachers to go on retreat every summer. Plan to spend significant time with the synoptic gospel for the coming year, perhaps several hours each morning for a week. Begin by reading the entire narrative from beginning to end in one sitting. The goal of this first reading is to grasp the overall movement of the story, not to become distracted by details.

You will have to make a few significant decisions before beginning this work. In year B, where does Mark end? Without getting bogged down in the concerns of textual criticism, I accept the consensus view that the original ending of Mark is at 16:8.[5] The so-called longer and shorter endings were added later by scribes dissatisfied with a story that ended with the women fleeing from the tomb in fear, unable to speak. They tried to clear up the confusion by adding what seemed to them more satisfying endings. However, I want to challenge preachers to consider *what is the meaning of a story that ends the way Mark ends?*

---

[5]For an informative summary of the problem, see Bruce M. Metzger, *Textual Commentary on the Greek New Testament,* 2d ed. (New York: United Bible Societies, 1995), 122–28.

In year C, you need to decide whether the gospel of Luke is to be read as a discrete narrative or as the first part of a larger narrative, Luke-Acts. While there has been considerable scholarly discussion of this very question, I leave it to the reader to reach his or her own conclusions. I have worked with the assumption that Luke-Acts is a single narrative in two parts.

This first reading is to be a spontaneous, even naïve, engagement with the text. As Fred Craddock describes the process,

> All faculties of mind and heart are open, with no concern for what one ought to think…This is the time to listen, think, feel, imagine, and ask. All responses should be jotted down; do not trust the memory or take time to weigh the merits of your thought.[6]

Above all, I encourage you to trust your own ability to read a story. Trust your own intuition. If a portion of the narrative raises questions, highlight those troubling points in the text. Those questions should be recorded and pondered. They should *not* be resolved by going immediately to commentaries and seeking the explanations of "experts." Your own questions are valuable, for they become the entry point into your homiletical reflection on specific sermon texts. Looking ahead, you will be able to exploit the problematic areas of the narrative; they can be used in the sermon to "upset the equilibrium."

To summarize, read the story-as-a-whole and let it work on your imagination. This is not the time to short-circuit your engagement with the story-as-story. Do not try to answer all the questions that surface. Allow the story to bother you, get under your skin, pique your curiosity, intrigue your imagination. Take advantage of the capacity of narrative to surprise you, to push you beyond the envelope of a settled vision of life and faith.

Conversing about the narrative. It will be productive, after your own imaginative engagement with the narrative, to participate in wider conversations. Such conversations may take the form of a lectionary study group composed of clergy in your community. You can also conduct such a conversation with a Bible study group in your own congregation. Such conversations are most valuable when

---

[6]Fred B. Craddock, *Preaching* (Nashville: Abingdon Press, 1985), 105–6.

participants are stimulated by the distinct perspectives, questions, and insights offered by each member of the group. Differing perspectives can serve as grist for the mill, to prompt reflection and exploration. It is hoped that they will prompt further reading in the narrative itself. The full benefit of conversing with others can occur only to the extent that you have done your own wrestling with the text and articulated your *own* questions.

This is also the point at which you can benefit from reading narrative studies of the gospel written by biblical scholars. It is important to reflect on the relationship of the working preacher and the biblical scholar. Narrative biblical critics can help the preacher by showing us how to engage in a close reading of a biblical narrative. Published literature represents the fruit of years of a scholar's sustained engagement with a gospel. The author is writing out of a comprehensive knowledge of the biblical narrative. Out of that familiarity can come insights that may not have occurred to the preacher. Such insights are not to be accepted uncritically. Their value consists of highlighting unnoticed places in a narrative world, of suggesting intriguing questions, of making surprising connections that you may find fruitful in your further reading. To summarize, the purpose of conversations with the scholarly literature is to stimulate your own imagination, not to resolve ambiguities or answer questions.

Recording questions and insights. This first reading of a biblical narrative will become the fertile ground for subsequent homiletical engagement with sermon texts. It is essential to find some way to record your questions and insights. The use of a notebook or journal may be a helpful discipline for some. Notes written in the margins of a Bible may work for others. Some may consider creating an artistic expression of their reading of the narrative. The production of a piece of artwork involves the right brain, engaging the intuitive, artistic self. This may encourage the preacher to approach the acts of interpretation and preaching with imagination.

From Text to Sermon

It is now Monday morning, six days before the sermon is to be delivered. The lectionary texts for next Sunday are open in front of you, but you are not starting from scratch. You have read the larger narrative during the previous summer. You have continued to work with that narrative as you have preached from it week after week. You have developed a basic but ongoing reading of the story-as-a-whole. That familiarity is the ground from which your creative engagement with the sermon text for next Sunday will come.

Brainstorming

The first step is to brainstorm all the possible ways that the sermon text is related to the larger narrative. Begin by reading the text out loud, perhaps several times from several translations, so that it is heard with the ears as well as seen with the eyes. As you continue to read and listen, look and listen for connections between the text and other portions of the larger narrative. What threads run through the fabric of the story-as-a-whole that surface in the text now before you? Record those recollections of the larger narrative. This is not the time to judge whether each possible connection that surfaces is appropriate or useful. The purpose of brainstorming is to help you relate imaginatively to the sermon text with the larger narrative in mind.

At the same time, it is important to verify that the recollections that surface do in fact come from the particular gospel you are reading. We are so accustomed to harmonizing the gospels that we tend to conflate their tellings of the story. For this reason, reread those portions of the gospel that come to mind to ensure that what you remember is actually part of that narrative. At the same time, keep your eyes open for neglected details in the text that may prompt further brainstorming.

Re-searching the Gospel

After encouraging the right brain to find imaginative connections, preachers can search the gospel more systematically for links between the sermon text and the larger narrative. The following are some ways to undertake that search.

- Look closely at the passages immediately preceding and following the pericope. What connections can you see? Sometimes the gospels will create a literary sandwich, beginning one story, telling a second, then returning and completing the first story. For example, the story of the unnamed woman who anointed Jesus at Bethany (Mk. 14:3–9) is ironically sandwiched between the account of Judas' arrangement with the chief priests and scribes to betray Jesus (Mk. 14:1–2, 10–11). This a clue that the author meant the two stories to be understood together.

- Look at significant words in the sermon text and locate other places in the larger narrative where those words are used. For example, Peter answers Jesus' question by saying, "You are the Messiah" (Mk. 8:29). Where else in Mark is the word *Messiah* (Greek, *Christos*) used? Take a look at those other passages and think about possible connections. By using a computerized concordance, you can search for words and phrases in a fraction of the time. Some programs can search the Greek and Hebrew texts, which is significant because translations often translate the same word differently at various places in the same book.

- Look at phrases in the sermon text that are repeated elsewhere in the narrative, either verbatim or with a slight variation. For example, James and John make a request of Jesus: "Grant us to sit, one at your right hand and one at your left, in your glory" (Mk. 10:37). The same phrase is found at one other place in Mark: "And with him they crucified two bandits, one on his right and one on his left" (Mk. 15:27) (the phrase in Greek is identical). What does this suggest about the places of glory sought by James and John?

- Look for images, themes, allusions, or rhetorical features in the text that are found elsewhere in the narrative. For example, Jesus speaks of his coming passion at Mark 8:31. Jesus will again speak of the passion at Mark 9:31 and Mark 10:33–34. How are the three passion predictions related? Or to give another example, the parable of the sower mentions four kinds of ground as representing four kinds of responses to Jesus' word. Where in the gospel can the reader find living examples of those responses?[7]

Being Open to Contemporary Images

In the course of brooding over the text, you may find images coming to you that have no direct connection with the biblical

---

[7]This is Mary Ann Tolbert's thesis in *Sowing the Gospel: Mark's World in Literary-Historical Perspective* (Minneapolis: Fortress Press, 1989).

narrative. In the course of opening your imagination to the text, be open to ideas, stories, metaphors, images, illustrations, and examples that come to you from the contemporary situation, from your life, from literature and movies, from popular culture, from wherever. Such ideas can come at any point in the process of crafting the sermon. Record them! The germ of an idea or an approach to the sermon may come from the images that arise in the course of reflecting on the text.

Establishing the Sermon's Plotline

At this point, you should get some distance from the text by spending time away from the sermon. Homiletical imagination can be well served by allowing the stories and images of the text to work in the subconscious mind. Pastoral visits, program planning, and administrative work beckon. Moreover, such work constitutes the context for Sunday's sermon. As Paul Scott Wilson advises, it is helpful to study the text "early in the week and view the events of the week through the lenses of the text. Parts of the story you had not noticed before will come alive for you."[8]   Of course, getting distance from the text and the sermon will prove to be productive only if you have begun your brooding early enough in the week.

When you come back to the sermon, perhaps on Tuesday afternoon or Wednesday morning, the task is different. The basic goal is now to conceptualize the sermon's basic plotline, its movement from disequilibrium to resolution. Eugene Lowry has done the theoretical work on plot-shaped preaching.[9] Lowry calls for sermons that are structured to exploit the rhetorical dynamics of narrative plot. The rhetorical appeal of a strong plot to a wide audience is based on emotional dynamics that are easily understood. Plots begin by hooking the reader, by raising a question. Who committed the murder? How will this love triangle turn out? Will Odysseus ever make it home to Ithaca? Modern readers keep turning the pages of a John Grisham novel for much the same reason as ancient hearers kept listening to Homer's *Odyssey*, to satisfy the narrative tension created

---

[8]Paul Scott Wilson, *Imagination of the Heart: New Understandings in Preaching* (Nashville: Abingdon Press, 1988), 68.

[9]Eugene L. Lowry, *The Homiletical Plot: The Sermon as Narrative Art Form* (Atlanta: John Knox Press, 1980), and *The Sermon: Dancing the Edge of Mystery* (Nashville: Abingdon Press, 1997).

in the plot's beginning. The skillfully constructed plot will keep the reader intrigued and will avoid resolving the tension until the very end. Stories whose endings we can figure out well in advance are not very satisfying.

The same is to happen in a plot-shaped sermon. The beginning of the sermon hooks the listener by "upsetting the equilibrium." It introduces and develops sermonic tension. For example, a sermon may begin by raising an ambiguity, considering a paradox, introducing a problem, or setting two ideas in tension. The end of the sermon "discloses the clue to resolution." It resolves the sermonic tension and fleshes out that resolution.

The key creative and imaginative moment in crafting the sermon involves asking a series of three questions. (1) Does the text in front of me, seen in light of the story-as-a-whole, *raise* a question or *answer* a question? (2) If the sermon text *raises* a question, where in the story-as-a-whole is that question answered? (3) If the sermon text *answers* a question, where in the larger story-as-a-whole is the question raised?

Although I will demonstrate this method fully in the following chapters, let me give an example. If you are preaching on the Marcan version of Peter's confession, consider whether the confession raises or answers a question. If the text raises a question (*did* Peter get it right?), where in Mark's story might we find a perspective on what it means to get it right? If the text answers a question (Peter *did* get it right!), where in Mark is the question answered by Peter raised?

It is at this point that the brainstorming done earlier in the week becomes useful. You have been thinking about the sermon text as it relates to the whole narrative. The question that the sermon text raises (or answers) is most likely the fruit of your brainstorming. Moreover, the narrative threads that you have uncovered in your brainstorming will probably prove to be fruitful places to find either the question to the text's answer or the answer to the text's question.

The goal of addressing these questions is to establish the sermon's plotline. The sermon begins by posing the question raised by the biblical narrative, then moves inductively toward the answer suggested by the biblical narrative. The sermon text provides one of those key moments; the other moment is to be found elsewhere in the larger narrative.

Weaving the Sermon

Having established the basic plotline of the sermon, you are now ready to weave the sermon.[10] Your brainstorming has given you a page or more of notes containing potential threads to be woven into the sermon. Some of these threads come from the biblical story-as-a-whole. They consist of connections between the sermon text and the larger narrative. Other threads consist of stories, metaphors, illustrations, and images from the contemporary world. It is likely that you have *far* more material than you would ever want to incorporate in a single sermon. Find a way to save this material for future use!

Weaving a sermon is a craft, not a science. There is no one right way to do this. This book contains a number of sample sermons. These should not be taken as a prescription for how to write a sermon, only as examples of ways in which sermons might be crafted. I encourage preachers to develop their own imaginations and creativity, to expose themselves to the creative efforts of other preachers, to participate in study groups with other preachers, to take part in continuing education events, and to read some of the many books on preaching that contemporary homileticians have written. Some suggested books can be found in the Bibliography.

Preaching the Sermon

Three facts about sermons need to be considered. First, a sermon is an event. A sermon is not the words on a page. It is the event of proclaiming a message. Words are spoken by the preacher and heard by the worshiping assembly. It is hoped that in the course of the event, the presence of God is encountered.

Second, a sermon is preached to a particular community. The community to which you will proclaim the word should be in your consciousness throughout the entire process just described. The members of the church are in your mind when you go on retreat and read the gospel from beginning to end. They are there when you brood over the text and in your brainstorming. Above all, the community should be present in your consciousness when you think about questions the text raises. Those questions arise from your people's own quest for faith and wholeness, from the missional

---

[10]This is the metaphor introduced by Christine M. Smith. See *Weaving the Sermon: Preaching in a Feminist Perspective* (Louisville, Ky.: Westminster/John Knox Press, 1989).

challenges facing your church, and from the pain of your community and nation. Those questions articulate the church's hunger to hear God's good news for a hurting world.

A sermon, finally, is an *oral* event. It is a form of communication that will be *heard*, not *read,* just as the gospels were. Throughout the process of crafting the sermon, keep in mind that your sermon will be heard. This will have implications not so much for the content of your message but for the way in which that content is communicated. We can learn from the evangelists themselves. Matthew did not include a treatise on showing mercy; he told the parable of the sheep and the goats. Mark did not exhort his congregation about the unfinished business of proclaiming the good news; he concluded his story in such a way that his hearers knew that if the good news was going to be told, they would have to do the telling. Luke did not give a lecture on the inclusiveness of God's love; he told story after story in which God's love was shown to and by women, Samaritans, tax collectors, Gentiles...those on the margins.

Preaching at its best is a joyful occasion in which the biblical story is told—and heard—and God is encountered in the event. That is at the heart of my concern that the church's preaching reclaim the narratives of the Bible. Narrative is a powerful medium. God is revealed through the events of the Bible and encountered through telling the stories of those events. That conviction is the reason for this book. It is an experiment with new ways of reading the synoptic narratives, new ways to tell the stories of Jesus.

2

Reading and Preaching
the Gospel of Mark

In the first half of this chapter, "Reading Mark's Gospel," I develop an overview of the Marcan narrative. In the second half of the chapter, "Preaching Mark's Gospel," I discuss how I constructed a particular sermon that arises from this reading of Mark. With this preview in mind, there are two ways readers might use this overview of Mark.

First, the reader can read this material to find out how I got from my reading of Mark's story-as-a-whole to a particular sermon on a particular text. Having developed a reading of Mark, I brainstormed narrative links between the confession pericope and the larger story, then wove those threads into a sermon that related the confession to the whole Marcan narrative. This chapter can be seen as documentation of my journey from text to sermon.

However, the material is more broadly useful. Although not intended as a substitute for the preacher's own engagement with Mark, the preacher can use this overview as an orientation to Mark's story-as-a-whole and to the questions the story raises. This may be particularly helpful, first, when preachers "go on retreat" with Mark during the summer before lectionary year B. You might reread the overview *after* first reading Mark yourself. It is hoped that it will raise questions that you can explore in the biblical text. Second, in the course of preparing a sermon on a Marcan text, you might use this overview to jog your memory of the story-as-a-whole. You may find yourself wrestling with possible connections between that text and the larger story: How does that passage fit into Mark's plot? How does Mark characterize figures who appear in the passage? Who was the reader Mark had in mind? This chapter offers one reading of such issues. Finally, you can use this material as a resource when teaching Bible studies in the local church. Laity have, in my experience, shown genuine interest in narrative approaches to the gospels. This overview is intended to be accessible to laity who are interested in biblical narrative but may not have technical training in biblical scholarship.

Reading Mark's Gospel

The gospel of Mark, with its ending that raises rather than resolves narrative tension, is a story that intrigues its readers. Its telling of the story of Jesus begins with John the Baptist preaching repentance in the Judean wilderness and ends with the women fleeing silently from the empty tomb. There are many ways to approach this narrative fruitfully. I will follow four narrative themes as they run through Mark's gospel.

(1) One thread concerns the identity of Jesus. While the reader knows from the opening verse precisely who Jesus is, characters in the story are in the dark. They grapple with the question, Who is Jesus? Readers, watching this struggle, wonder what it means to confess Jesus rightly.

(2) A second thread deals with Jesus' career. His ministry begins as an amazing success story. Disciples follow, the sick are healed, and the crowds are astonished at his teaching...but the success story soon becomes a passion story.

(3) A third thread centers on the role of the disciples. They are quick to follow but slow to understand what Jesus is all about. Each of the Twelve fails in the end.

(4) A final thread involves the female followers of Jesus. Present throughout the story in the background, they emerge from the shadows in the narrative's conclusion and serve as models of faith and discipleship.

The Identity of Jesus

Who is Jesus? Who in the story knows who Jesus is? Does everyone who correctly identifies Jesus understand who he is? Does anyone understand who Jesus is? Mark's story raises these questions and encourages the reader to wonder about them.

Insight for the reader. The issue of Jesus' identity comes to the fore at the narrative's very beginning. The opening sentence of the gospel declares, "The beginning of the good news of Jesus Christ, the Son of God" (1:1). This clear, unambiguous statement of who Jesus is is read by the reader, but this information is not provided to any of the characters in the narrative.

Though the narrative opens with a moment of complete clarity for the reader, such clarity is lacking within the world of Mark's story. John the Baptist recognizes the protagonist (who is not yet on the narrative scene) as "one who is more powerful than I" (1:7). However, there is no uptake to this apparently public proclamation within the narrative. The narrative is silent concerning who, if anyone, heard John's proclamation or how it was received by those who may have heard it. Although John recognizes, at least partially, who Jesus is, he is removed from the story at 1:14.

Jesus' identity is stated for a second time at the baptism. The reader overhears the voice that came from heaven: "You are my Son, the Beloved; with you I am well pleased" (1:11). The narrative again is silent concerning who, if anyone, heard this voice. The explicit sense of the words is that they are spoken directly to Jesus. Again, there is no uptake by any of the characters in the story to these words. In terms of their practical effect in Mark's narrative world, these words are heard only by Jesus and by the reader.

Later in the narrative, Jesus is identified in similar fashion. A voice speaks out of the cloud at the transfiguration. "This is my Son, the Beloved; listen to him!" (9:7). While these words seem to be spoken to Peter, James, and John, they have no apparent effect upon them. The disciples fail to listen to or accept Jesus' predictions about his own death and their own falling away. In addition, they fail to heed Jesus' teaching about the nature of discipleship. In practical terms, the voice speaks out of the clouds for the reader's benefit.

Recognized by demons. Another feature of the story soon becomes apparent. Jesus *is* recognized by certain characters in the story, by demons and by the demon-possessed. A man with an unclean spirit recognizes Jesus in the synagogue at Nazareth: "What have you to do with us, Jesus of Nazareth? Have you come to destroy us? I know who you are, the Holy One of God." Jesus' response is to rebuke (*epitimao*) the demon and command it, "Be silent" (1:25). The worshipers in the synagogue respond to the authority with which Jesus teaches but *not* to the content of the demon's statement. The reader wonders if the worshipers heard what the demon said.

The thread resurfaces when the narrative provides a summary statement of Jesus' ministry. The narrator states that "whenever the unclean spirits saw [Jesus], they fell down before him and shouted, 'You are the Son of God!' But he sternly rebuked [*epitimao*] them not to make him known" (3:11–12, author trans.).[1]

The story of the Gerasene demoniac follows the same thread. The demoniac, seeing Jesus from a distance, runs and bows down before him, shouting "at the top of his voice, 'What have you to do with me, Jesus, Son of the Most High God?'" (5:7). Jesus silences the many demons by sending them into a herd of swine. The demon-possessed swine destroy themselves by running off a cliff into the sea, where they are drowned.

Questions about Jesus' identity. While Jesus is recognized by demons whom he rebukes to silence, the human characters in the story find themselves questioning who Jesus is and why Jesus acts in the way he does.

- What is this? A new teaching—with authority! He commands even the unclean spirits, and they obey him. (1:27)
- Why does this fellow speak in this way? It is blasphemy! Who can forgive sins but God alone? (2:7)
- Why does he eat with tax collectors and sinners? (2:16)
- Why do John's disciples and the disciples of the Pharisees fast, but your disciples do not fast? (2:18)
- Look, why are they doing what is not lawful on the sabbath? (2:24)
- Where did this man get all this? What is this wisdom that has been given to him? What deeds of power are being done by his hands! Is not this the carpenter, the son of Mary and the

---

[1]It is not possible to render *epitimao* exactly into English. I have chosen to use the verb "to rebuke" consistently, even in cases such as this where it is grammatically incorrect. No other English word can better convey the sense of *epitimao*, which is to issue a rebuke and a command.

brother of James and Joses and Judas and Simon, and are not his sisters here with us? (6:2–3)

- Why do your disciples not live according to the tradition of the elders, but eat with defiled hands? (7:5)

Opinion begins to cluster around three tentative conclusions as to Jesus' identity: "Some were saying, 'John the baptizer has been raised from the dead; and for this reason these powers are at work in him.' But others said, 'It is Elijah.' And others said, 'It is a prophet, like one of the prophets of old.'" Of these options Herod concludes that "John, whom I beheaded, has been raised" (6:14–16).

The same three tentative conclusions are named when Jesus asks his disciples who the public thinks he is:

> Jesus went on with his disciples to the villages of Caesarea Philippi; and on the way he asked his disciples, "Who do people say that I am?" And they answered him, "John the Baptist; and others, Elijah; and still others, one of the prophets." He asked them, "But who do you say that I am?" Peter answered him, "You are the Messiah." And he rebuked [*epitimao*] them not to tell anyone about him. (8:27–30, author trans.)

Peter identifies Jesus as the Messiah. This is the first time in the story that a human character recognizes what the reader and the demons have known from the beginning. Jesus replies to Peter's confession in the same way that he has responded to the demons who recognized him (1:25; 3:12). Peter and the disciples are rebuked to silence.

Ironic recognitions of Jesus. The passion narrative contains a number of ironic recognitions of Jesus by his enemies. The first comes from the lips of the high priest who asks, "You are the Messiah, the Son of the Blessed One?" (author translation). Jesus responds with an emphatic "I am." Having asked for and received Jesus' only unambiguous confirmation within Mark that he is the Messiah, the high priest categorizes Jesus' answer as blasphemy (14:61–63).

Jesus is then called "the King of the Jews" by Pilate (15:2, 9, 12), by the soldiers who mock him (15:8), and by means of the inscription on the cross (15:26). King of the Jews is a messianic title with political implications. It is ironic that these words come first from the lips of Pilate, the personal manifestation of Roman rule in Jerusalem. He speaks these words to Jesus while Jesus is on trial before him. Even while referring to Jesus as "King of the Jews," Pilate hands him over to be crucified.

The soldiers call Jesus "King of the Jews" while engaging in a mock coronation. The whole cohort is called together for the ceremony. They robe Jesus in purple, crown him (with thorns), salute him ("Hail, King of the Jews"), and kneel down in homage to him.

The inscription upon the cross contains the words "The King of the Jews." The irony is that this public affirmation constitutes the charge for which Jesus is being crucified. It is intended, according to the narrator, as a summary "of the charge against him" (15:26), as a statement of the capital offense for which this man is being executed.

The narrator describes the attitude of those who saw Jesus dying on the cross. Those passing by "derided him" (15:29), the chief priests and scribes "were…mocking him among themselves" (15:31), and others being crucified with Jesus "taunted him" (15:32). It is in such a context that Jesus is referred to by chief priests and scribes as "the Messiah, the King of the Jews" (15:32, author trans.). This too is an explicitly ironic recognition of Jesus from the point of view of Mark's readers.

What of the Roman centurion who, upon Jesus' death, calls him "a son of God" (15:39)? Scholars espouse a full range of possible interpretations, some seeing this as a straightforward affirmation of Jesus' identity (Gundry), others viewing the centurion as the exceptional soldier (Malbon), and still others reading the centurion's words as a taunt (Juel).[2] I read the centurion's statement as ironic, coming as it does at the climax of a series of ironic recognitions.

A series of flawed recognition scenes. By following the narrative thread of recognition, the reader is presented with a series of flawed recognition scenes. Jesus is recognized by the demons, but surely the demons do not represent what it means to confess Jesus. Jesus is recognized by Peter, but Peter will subsequently deny that he knows Jesus. Jesus is recognized by his enemies who speak correct titles, but these confessions can only be described as highly ironic. Is there any ultimate recognition of Jesus in the story world of Mark?

---

[2]See Robert H. Gundry, *Mark: A Commentary on His Apology for the Cross* (Grand Rapids, Mich.: Eerdmans, 1993), 950; Elizabeth Struthers Malbon, "Fallible Followers: Men and Women in the Gospel of Mark," *Semeia* 28 (1983): 31; and Juel, *A Master of Surprise*, 74, n. 7.

Homiletical reflection. The gospel of Mark is filled with characters who identify Jesus using "correct" titles yet fail to demonstrate what it means to believe in and follow Jesus. Demons, enemies, and disciples all speak orthodox words, but correct words themselves do not ensure that the speaker is a person of faith. Marcan sermons can encourage the church to question whether "correct doctrine" is the real bottom line of Christianity. Orthodoxy without love, humility, and insight turns out to be a rather hollow expression of faith in Mark's story.

From Success Story to Passion Story: The Career of Jesus

The plot of the gospel of Mark consists of two movements with Peter's confession—at the center of the gospel—constituting a major turning point. The first movement begins in the wilderness and culminates at the high point of the confession. The second movement begins at the confession and moves toward the empty tomb. The tone of the two movements is quite different.

First movement: toward the confession. The first movement portrays the early career of Jesus as an apparent success story. Following Jesus' announcement that "the kingdom of God is at hand" (1:15, RSV), there follows a description of Jesus' successful ministry in which the reality of the inbreaking kingdom is seen. Jesus calls followers, and they follow without question. Jesus heals the sick, casts out demons, forgives sins, feeds the multitudes, and overcomes the forces of nature. Large crowds are attracted to him and follow him wherever he goes. Jesus' popularity engenders controversy, but there is as yet no indication that he cannot overcome his opponents.

Jesus' activities provoke questions, especially from his opponents, concerning the content, manner, and source of his teachings and practices. Suspense is building among the characters within Mark's story world. They ask a series of questions concerning the identity of the protagonist. The reader already knows who Jesus is, having been given this information by the narrator at the very beginning of the book (1:1). The demons also know who Jesus is (1:24; 3:11; 5:7). However, human characters within the narrative remain in the dark. They ask questions and come to varying conclusions as to Jesus' identity (3:22; 6:14–16).

It is interesting that, in a narrative so full of dialogue, Jesus' disciples are relatively silent. The first four disciples leave their professions and their families without speaking a word (1:16–20). When the disciples do speak, their words typically betray a lack of perception

(4:38; 5:31; 6:35–38; 8:4–5, 16–20). The silent disciples first voice the question of Jesus' identity at 4:41 in response to Jesus' calming the sea: "Who then is this, that even the wind and the sea obey him?" The disciples come again to the fore in 8:27–30 when Jesus asks them two questions: "Who do people say that I am?" and "Who do you say that I am?" For the first time within the narrative proper, a human character states what the readers and the demons have known from the beginning: Peter says, "You are the Messiah" (8:29).

The movement toward the empty tomb. Peter's confession constitutes a turning point in at least three different ways. First, the ensuing narrative will plainly indicate that the gospel's meaning cannot be construed in terms of a simple success story that celebrates the miracles of Jesus. The narrative that follows redefines the nature of Jesus' ministry. It is stated explicitly that Jesus will face suffering (8:31; 9:12), rejection (8:31; 12:10), betrayal (9:31), humiliation (10:34), and death (8:31; 9:31; 10:34).

Second, the confession represents a turning point in the reader's estimation of Peter and the disciples. Although the reader has been led to question the disciples' perceptivity, Peter's correct assertion of Jesus' identity encourages the reader to hope that the disciples are finally beginning to see. Such a hopeful outcome, however, is immediately quashed. On hearing Jesus' first prophecy of the passion (8:31), Peter begins to rebuke this new word. Jesus in turn rebukes Peter and calls him "Satan" (8:32–33). On two more occasions, Jesus repeats the prophecy of his passion (9:31–32; 10:33–34). Each time, the disciples respond in ways inappropriate to the words just spoken (9:33–34; 10:35–37). For the first time in the narrative, there is a hint of failure as the disciples fail to exorcise a demon (9:17–18). By the end of this broad movement, Judas will have betrayed Jesus, Peter will have denied him, and the rest of the Twelve will have deserted him. The disciples will have been thoroughly discredited in the view of the reader.

Third, Jesus has reached the northernmost limit of his travels at the time of Peter's confession. Caesarea Philippi is the farthest distance he will ever be away from Jerusalem. The plot begins to move in a new direction geographically. Jesus moves southward through Galilee to the regions of Judea and trans-Jordan. He journey takes him toward Jerusalem. He enters the city and challenges his opponents. His three prophecies of the passion are fulfilled in precise detail as he is arrested and crucified.

This second broad movement of the narrative concludes at the empty tomb. Mark has a surprise ending. There is no appearance in this story of the resurrected Jesus. Neither is there a triumphant conclusion for the disciples. The only characters on Mark's narrative stage at the end are the women. The gospel ends with an announcement of the resurrection but no appearance, with witnesses who hear the announcement but run wordlessly from the tomb.

Homiletical reflection. Mark, unlike the other evangelists, does not tell a triumphalistic story. The narrative's ambiguous ending leaves the reader with many open questions: What did Jesus accomplish? Did the women ever speak? Were the disciples ever rehabilitated? Marcan sermons can use this feature of the story. Triumphalism can have a rather hollow ring for listeners who live in an increasingly secular age. Our congregations have a natural affinity for Mark's narrative world, a world in which much seed is scattered and little comes to full flower, a world in which the church is struggling to assert its agenda in the face of powerful and amoral forces, a world in which even the call to speak can seem a frightening prospect. Mark's story gives preachers a means to speak to the struggles that today's church faces.

The Rise and Fall of the Disciples

Paralleling the two movements in Jesus' career is the status of the disciples in the story. During the movement to the confession, the reader's perception of the disciples is on the rise. During the movement to the empty tomb, the reader's estimation of the disciples is on the decline.

The rise of the disciples. I will focus my discussion of the male disciples on the role of Simon Peter in the gospel of Mark. The reader first encounters Simon Peter at the beginning of Jesus' ministry. Peter is presented consistently as preeminent among the disciples and is more fully characterized than the other members of the Twelve. Simon is the first disciple called by Jesus in the narrative. The group following Jesus in the earliest stages of his ministry is referred to as "Simon and his companions" (1:36). When Jesus goes up the mountain, appoints the Twelve, and designates them as apostles, Simon heads the list. The narrator refers on several occasions to a group of three or four who may represent an inner circle among the disciples; Peter's name appears consistently at the head of this group

(1:16–19; 5:37; 9:2; 13:3–4). Peter often speaks on behalf of the entire group (8:29; 9:5; 11:14, 20, 31).

Simon Peter's status is on the rise in the first movement of the gospel. When first encountered by the reader, Simon is a fisherman at work with his brother Andrew beside the Sea of Galilee. While he is an individual possessing relatively modest social status in first-century agrarian society, what is of significance is his status within the narrative world of Mark's gospel. Mark's story describes the formation of a new group within the larger society, a new society with an entirely different hierarchy of values.[3] In Mark's world, the voice speaking from heaven belongs to the one with the highest status, God. That voice confers upon Jesus the status of "my Son, the Beloved" (1:11). Passing along by the sea, Jesus calls Simon to follow him (1:17), conveying on him the status of being Jesus' follower. Jesus accepts an invitation to be a guest in Simon's home in 1:29–34, further enhancing Simon's status. His status within the group increases further when, in the course of appointing the Twelve in 3:13–19, Simon is the first disciple named and receives a new name from Jesus. When Jesus enters the home of Jairus, a leader of the synagogue, to heal Jairus' daughter, Jesus allows only Peter, James, and John to enter the house with him, further enhancing the honor of these three.

Mark 8:27–30, the account of Peter's confession, can be read in terms of challenge and riposte, an opportunity for honor to be gained or lost. The first question, "Who do people say that I am?" is a relatively nonthreatening question. An answer to that question requires merely the passing on of information the disciples may have heard. This inquiry is followed by a second, more direct question, "Who do you say that I am?" This question is a challenge to the disciples' honor. A correct answer would bring honor to the disciple answering this challenge, while an incorrect answer would bring shame. Peter accepts this challenge to his honor and answers,

---

[3]An excellent discussion of the concept of honor is found in Bruce J. Malina and Jerome H. Neyrey, "Honor and Shame in Luke-Acts: Pivotal Values of the Mediterranean World," in *The Social World of Luke-Acts: Models for Interpretation*, ed. Jerome H. Neyrey (Peabody, Mass.: Hendrickson, 1991), 25–65. Honor, the most important commodity in Mediterranean society, is gained or lost through challenge and riposte. Issuing an invitation to dinner is, for example, a challenge to the recipient's honor, and honor is gained if that invitation is accepted (34, 52). Simon's inclusion in an inner circle also enhances his honor (32–34).

"You are the Messiah" (8:29). The reader, who has known from 1:1 that Jesus is the Messiah, can only assume that Peter has answered correctly. By virtue of a successful riposte to Jesus' challenge, Peter's honor has risen to its highest point in the narrative. At no point in Mark's narrative does Peter possess greater status than at the moment he speaks the words of his confession.

The fall of the disciples. Peter's fall begins precisely at this point; 8:30 is a moment of reversal not only for Jesus but for Peter and the Twelve. Jesus' response to Peter's confession must come as a shock to the reader. Jesus rebukes (*epitimao*) Peter to remain silent, the same response he made to the demons when they shouted out Jesus' identity (1:25; 3:12).

The three passion predictions. The first of three prophecies of the passion follows immediately. Peter responds forcefully to Jesus' talk of his suffering, rejection, and death by rebuking (*epitimao*) Jesus (8:32). Jesus, in turn, rebukes (*epitimao*) Peter and names him "Satan" (8:33). Because of this series of rebukes, what appeared initially to be a successful riposte to Jesus' challenge becomes a catastrophe. Robert Fowler has characterized this episode as "the fiercest confrontation imaginable between a teacher and his pupils."[4] Peter has lost honor in the exchange.

Each of the three passion prophecies sets up the fall of Peter and the Twelve. The first prophecy states that the Messiah will suffer and be rejected, a notion that Peter rebukes. By implication, Peter is also rejecting the notion that to be a disciple may involve embracing suffering. Jesus' teaching that anyone who wants to follow him must deny himself or herself is a haunting foreshadowing of what is to come. In a moment of crisis, Peter will be unable to deny himself by confessing Jesus; rather, he will deny Jesus three times (14:66–72). The episode that follows the first prophecy, the healing of the mute boy who "foams and grinds his teeth and becomes rigid" when trying to speak (9:18), likewise foreshadows Peter's inability to speak the truth when confronted by the servant girl.

The second and central prophecy states that the Son of Man is to be betrayed into human hands, referring to what Judas will do

---

[4]Robert M. Fowler, *Let the Reader Understand: Reader-Response Criticism and the Gospel of Mark* (Minneapolis: Fortress Press, 1991), 71.

later in the narrative. The story that shortly follows, Jesus' encounter with the rich young man, alludes to scenes both earlier and later in the narrative. It reminds the reader of the seed sown among thorns that is choked by "the lure of wealth" (4:19). It foreshadows Judas' betrayal of Jesus in return for money (14:11).

The third prophecy of the passion details the physical affronts the Messiah will endure. He will be mocked, spit upon, and flogged, the victim of public humiliation and disgrace. James and John respond to this prediction with an incongruous request, that they be seated at Jesus' right and left in his glory, the two positions of highest honor. The irony of this request is revealed later in the narrative when the narrator uses, for a second time, the phrase "on his right and on his left": two bandits are crucified along with Jesus, one on either side (15:27). The places at Jesus' side so coveted by James and John are places not of honor, but of shame. As Jesus goes on to teach his disciples, a Christian leader is not to aspire to the status of Gentile rulers, a "great one" high in status, but is to accept the role of a *diakonos*, a servant, a position seen by the world as one of low status.

The sequence of three passion prophecies has a marked effect on the reader. It functions to lower the status of Peter and the Twelve in the reader's estimation. In the course of rejecting and misunderstanding what Jesus has said, the Twelve lose honor.

The passion story. The three passion prophecies set up the eventual "fall" of Peter and the Twelve. The passion prophecies focus the reader on the disciples' inability to understand or accept that the Messiah must endure suffering. The disciples are scandalized at the notion that Jesus will accept the ultimate loss of honor, capital punishment. It is not surprising that the disciples are unable to see their own discipleship in light of Jesus' messiahship. The passion predictions prepare the reader for the failure of the disciples, a failure that is realized in the story of the passion.

The first phase of the disciples' fall involves Judas' betrayal. The chief priests are "looking for a way to arrest Jesus by stealth and kill him" (14:1–2). Judas offers to betray Jesus to them in 14:10–11. The plotline resumes at the passover table. Jesus says to the Twelve, "Truly I tell you, one of you will betray me" (14:18). Emphasis is put on the fact that Jesus' betrayer is one of the Twelve; it is stated three times that the betrayer will be "one of the Twelve" (14:10, 20, 43). The betrayal is accomplished at 14:43–46 when Judas identifies Jesus to the crowd by kissing him. He loses all honor by doing the unthinkable, by betraying the leader of his group.[5]

The second phase of the disciples' fall is introduced when Jesus says to them on the Mount of Olives that "all will be scandalized" (14:27, author trans.). The same Greek verb, *skandalizo*, has been used to describe the fate of the seed sown in rocky ground; "when trouble or persecution arises on account of the word, immediately they are scandalized" (4:17, author trans.). The disciples object to Jesus' prediction; first Peter, then each of the Twelve asserts that they would rather die with Jesus than betray him. Despite their brave assertions, Jesus' prediction will be realized shortly. Upon Jesus' arrest, "all of them deserted him and fled" (14:50).

The final phase of the disciples' fall takes place with the reader's attention focused on Peter, the last remaining male disciple. Jesus makes an emphatic and detailed prediction that Peter will deny him three times. Peter's denial becomes all the more agonizing because the narrative pace slows at this point. Peter follows Jesus "at a distance" to the place of the trial. As the trial proceeds, Peter is approached by a female slave who challenges him: "You also were with Jesus, the man from Nazareth." Peter accepts a challenge from this woman near the absolute bottom of the social scale, thus losing honor.[6] He is unable to tell the truth, insisting instead, "I do not know or understand what you are talking about." He walks away from the female slave, but she approaches Peter and challenges him a second time. "This man is one of them," she says. Peter again denies the truth that she has spoken. Yet a third time, answering the challenge of a bystander, Peter denies his association with Jesus. The rooster crows a second time, fulfilling Jesus' prediction to the last detail. The reader sees Peter for the last time in the gospel, broken and crying. Having once been the first of Jesus' followers, he has lost all honor in losing a challenge from a female slave.

Homiletical reflection. Mark's characterization of the disciples has clear implications on how to preach from Marcan texts. We cannot use the Marcan disciples as unambiguous models of faith. The Marcan call stories are not a good vehicle for speaking about conversion.

---

[5]Malina and Neyrey, "Honor and Shame," 32, 34, 41.
[6]According to Malina and Neyrey, one accepts challenges only from one's social equals.

Peter's confession cannot be taken as a straightforward celebration of his christological insight. The disciples in Mark do not portray what it means to develop in one's personal faith or to grow in one's discipleship. On the other hand, Mark's story does offer the preacher an opportunity to explore the difficulties of discipleship, to consider the real struggles involved in following the way of Jesus, and to contemplate our capacity to fall short of our own aspirations. When we preach from Mark, we can speak a compassionate word of grace to contemporary followers of Jesus who have known failure in their discipleship: You *can* pick up the cross that you dropped and follow again on the way.

The Women Emerge: The Silent, Nameless Followers of Jesus

The role of the disciples is quite familiar to the readers of Mark, for these disciples have positions of prominence in Mark's narrative world. They receive frequent mention in the gospel. They all have names. They are often vocal. They are exclusively male.

There is another group of followers of Jesus much less familiar to readers of Mark, for the story of these disciples is told in a muted voice. These characters rarely appear in the narrative. Most remain nameless throughout the gospel; the reader will finally learn the names of three of them at 15:40, sixteen verses before the story's end. Though they remain virtually voiceless, their actions are paradigms of discipleship. They are, by the way, the only group of characters in the gospel who receive Jesus' consistent and unambiguous affirmation. They are women.

MODELS OF DISCIPLESHIP

Framing the entire gospel, we find accounts of the women who followed and served Jesus. We encounter women from the very beginning of Jesus' ministry. The mother-in-law of Simon is the first woman who receives mention in Mark.

> As soon as they left the synagogue, they entered the house of Simon and Andrew, with James and John. Now Simon's mother-in-law was in bed with a fever, and they told him about her at once. He came and took her by the hand and lifted her up. Then the fever left her, and she began to serve them [*diakoneo*]. (1:29–31)

The reader notices the passive role of the woman in this story. The narrator neither gives her a name of her own nor permits her to speak for herself. Instead, the men approach Jesus on her behalf. Upon being healed, she began to serve the men. This could well be read as a reflection of the androcentric view that the place of women was to serve men. While not disagreeing with this observation, I would argue as well that Simon's mother-in-law portrays what is in Mark's world the model of true discipleship.

We also encounter women at the conclusion of Jesus' ministry.

> There were also women looking on from a distance; among them were Mary Magdalene, and Mary the mother of James the younger and of Joses, and Salome. These used to follow him and provided [*diakoneo*] for him when he was in Galilee; and there were many other women who had come up with him to Jerusalem. (15:40–41)

The verb *diakoneo*, to serve, is used five times in the gospel of Mark. In 1:13, Jesus is in the wilderness and the angels are serving him. In the two passages just mentioned, both Simon's mother-in-law and the group of women served Jesus in Galilee. The other two instances of the verb's use are found at 10:45. James and John have asked for seats of honor; in reply Jesus says, "the Son of Man came not to *be served* but *to serve*" (emphasis added). The noun *diakonos* is used in 9:35; Jesus says that "whoever wants to be first must be last of all and *servant* of all" (emphasis added).

In Mark's narrative, *serving* is the posture of the Son of Man and of the true disciple. The male disciples have been unable to accept such a role. It contradicts their assumption that the highest value is honor, as is culturally determined. In Mark's story of Jesus, Jesus and the women portray a model of true discipleship, a model that scandalizes the male disciples.

The moment of reversal. Mark 15:40 is a moment of reversal for the female followers of Jesus.[7] The male disciples are now totally absent from the stage, having fled in the face of the scandal of the cross. The positive involvement of the women, only alluded to earlier, now becomes realized. First, the women are given names. Second, this turning point initiates a chain of events involving the women.

---

[7]Winsome Munro, "Women Disciples in Mark?" *Semeia* 28 (1983): 225–41.

Third, the visual perspective of the narrator shifts. At 15:40 we are no longer facing the cross but looking away from the cross. There on the horizon we see the women "looking on from a distance." Note that their position relative to Jesus is identical to that of Peter at 14:54. As Joseph of Arimathea buries Jesus' body, two of the women, Mary Magdalene and Mary, come closer and observe the burial itself.

In 16:1–8, Mary Magdalene, Mary, and Salome come to the tomb to anoint Jesus' body. Far from being scandalized by the crucified one, they intend to touch the corpse, to honor the one whom society has deprived of all honor. They are presented as entering the tomb. They have become "insiders." These female counterparts of Peter, James, and John never betrayed or denied Jesus. They were not scandalized by the events of 15:1–39. They alone of Jesus' followers faced the crucifixion. They alone planned to anoint Jesus' body. As Malbon affirms, "within the Marcan story, only the women follow Jesus to the end."[8]

Models of Faith

Framing the passion story are two accounts that feature silent women who anoint Jesus. These women speak not through their words but through their actions. The first account, 14:3–9, appears at the beginning of the passion story. It involves a silent, unnamed woman who enters the house of Simon the leper. Never speaking a word, she breaks open a jar containing a costly ointment of nard and pours its contents on Jesus' head. Her shameless and apparently wasteful action becomes the focal point of the anger of the onlookers. Jesus, however, defends her for having performed a good work, for having "anointed my body beforehand for its burial" (14:8). This action constitutes a silent confession that Jesus is the Messiah, the Anointed One. Jesus responds to her act with the most unambiguous statement of praise directed toward anyone in Mark's narrative world. "Truly I tell you, wherever the good news is proclaimed in the whole world, what she has done will be told in remembrance of her" (14:9).

The passion story concludes with a second story of the women who followed Jesus (15:40—16:8). This account informs the reader

---

[8]Malbon, "Fallible Followers," 42.

that many women who had followed Jesus have watched his cruci-fixion. We are told the names of three of those women, Mary Magdalene, Mary, and Salome, who form a female counterpart to the inner group of the male disciples, Peter, James, and John. The three women make plans to come to the tomb to anoint Jesus' body. Like the unnamed woman of 14:3–9, these women are making a silent confession of Jesus as the Messiah, the Anointed One.

What does it mean in Mark's story to recognize Jesus? Jesus is recognized not by those characters who speak christological titles but by characters who speak through their actions. Framing the passion story, the women affirm through their hands that Jesus is the Messiah, the Anointed One.

Homiletical reflection. Mark's story gives preachers the opportunity to speak of the role of women who have been silenced both in the text and in the tradition. Though they live in the margins of the text, the female followers of Jesus are the characters who embody the values of discipleship. They are willing to embrace the one the world rejected, to approach the shame of the cross, to accept the word that messiahship and discipleship entails suffering. Marcan sermons can highlight that faithful actions, not correct words, are the true mark of the disciple. Mark's story gives preachers a way to put flesh on Paul's theology of call (1 Cor. 1:26–29).

Who Is the Implied Reader of Mark?

For whom was the gospel of Mark originally intended? A typical reading has hypothesized that the gospel was written for a community of Christians in Rome about to face persecution. The purpose of the book was to comfort that community and encourage it to remain faithful. Does such a reading make sense in light of the story we have before us? Mark's ending simply does not make sense if the purpose of the book was to comfort its readers. The Marcan ending does not comfort but rather unsettles the reader.

I am attracted to Donald Juel's understanding of Mark's implied reader. The narrative was addressed *not* to an impoverished and persecuted congregation but to an indifferent and unperceptive congregation. The implied reader is not poor and suffering but comfortable and complacent. Simon and Andrew were fishers. James and John not only owned a boat with their father but had an employee. Levi was a tax collector. These disciples are not characterized as living on the economic margins of society; they are portrayed as artisans.

Consider the threats to discipleship that are described in Mark's narrative world:

- The seed sown among thorns represents "the ones who hear the word, but the cares of the world, and the lure of wealth, and the desire for other things come in and choke the word" (4:18–19).
- The disciples argue about greatness (9:34).
- Jesus warns the disciples about wealth (10:23).
- James and John are concerned about positions of glory; Jesus warns them about imitating rulers of the Gentiles who "lord it over" their people (10:42–45).

Such challenges do not make sense for a suffering, persecuted, or impoverished audience. They make sense given a church that is fairly comfortable, given Christians who are concerned about their own status within the community, given church leaders who may be heavy-handed in asserting and exercising authority.

Consider as well the so-called little apocalypse (Mark 13). Though the disciples are impressed with the grandeur of the temple, indicating their materialistic values, Jesus warns them of hard times to come. They will be handed over to councils, beaten in synagogues, made to stand before governors and kings, brought to trial, and betrayed by parents and siblings (13:9–13). In the apocalyptic end times, they will endure everything that Jesus has endured in his passion. Or to put it another way, the church will face the same set of situations that once scandalized the disciples, the same dangers that once led the disciples to betray, deny, and flee from Jesus.

Consider that Jesus challenges the disciples to "keep awake" for the hour of trial (13:33, 35, 37). Despite Jesus' urgings, the disciples are unable to keep awake in their hour of trial. They repeatedly fall asleep in the garden of Gethsemane (14:34, 37, 38), an indication of their inability to face the challenges that lie ahead.

I thus read Mark as being written for a comfortable and complacent congregation. Mark's audience has been lulled into a false sense of security. They are asleep, unaware of dangers that lie ahead. Like the disciples in Mark's narrative, they have been taken in by the lure of wealth. Leaders within the church are concerned with the perks of their positions. They have bought into their culture's values: honor, power, and glory. They are scandalized by the values of Jesus: "whoever wishes to become great among you must be [your *diakonos*,] your servant" (10:43). Such a church cannot survive the challenges ahead.

Mark has therefore written a story in which such disciples fail. He has emphasized the scandalization of the Twelve. Jesus' inner circle of followers has bought into the wrong set of values. At the first sign of trouble they desert Jesus and run away. At the same time, the Marcan narrative affirms that the female followers of Jesus have embodied the same set of values that Jesus has lived. The women show their discipleship not through orthodox words but through faithful *diakonia*. Though silent throughout the story, their actions confess Jesus as the Anointed One. The women demonstrate the kind of discipleship the church needs in order to face the difficult times ahead. The narrative ends with unfinished business and an implicit challenge: If the good news is to be proclaimed, it is up to you, the readers, to embody the paradigm of discipleship demonstrated by the women and proclaim the good news by words and actions.

Preaching Mark's Gospel

The text before us is Mark 8:27–30, the Marcan account of Peter's confession. Prior to Sunday morning, the preacher will have engaged the Marcan narrative in a number of ways. First, I have recommended that preachers go on retreat with Mark in the summer preceding year B, read the story in one sitting, and record the questions that arise in this first reading of the text. Second, the preacher can engage in larger conversations around the text, reading what narrative biblical critics have written and taking part in group discussions about the gospel. Third, preachers will work with texts from Mark throughout year B. During the course of this sustained engagement with Mark, the preacher is developing a reading of the narrative. Moreover, the preacher will return to Mark every third year, having been engaged in the narrative worlds of Matthew and Luke in the subsequent years. The two years away from Mark can be productive, enabling the preacher to return to the Marcan narrative with new eyes.

Brainstorming and Researching the Gospel

We approach the text for next Sunday with an ongoing but still developing familiarity with Mark. Read the text out of that familiarity. Read it out loud and listen for connections with the larger story. A number of possibilities begin to emerge from an engagement with 8:27–30.

- Jesus' question concerning public perceptions of his identity has been prepared for by a series of questions from various human characters in the story. These questions have concerned Jesus' identity, his behavior, and his authority (1:27; 2:7, 16, 18, 24; 6:2–3; 7:5). Although the gospel has begun with a clear, unambiguous statement of Jesus' identity for the reader, such clarity is lacking among human characters within the narrative.
- The answers to Jesus' question "Who do people say that I am?" parallel the opinions offered in the context of Herod's hearing of Jesus.

Mark 6:14–16	**Mark 8:28–29**
"John the baptizer has been raised from the dead; and for this reason these powers are at work in him."	"John the Baptist;
But others said, "It is Elijah."	and others, Elijah;
And others said, "It is a prophet, like one of the prophets of old."	and still others, one of the prophets."
Herod: "John, whom I beheaded, has been raised."	Peter: "You are the Messiah."

Speculations about Jesus' identity are consistent in the reports made to Herod and Jesus. Given this set of possibilities, Herod chooses the first of the three opinions, concluding that "John, whom I beheaded, has been raised" (6:14–16). Pressed by Jesus for his opinion, Peter's answer represents a possibility not mentioned by the people: "You are the Messiah."

- Peter's answer consists of a formal title, *Christos*, Messiah. The preacher might look at the seven instances in the Marcan narrative where this title is used (1:1; 8:29; 9:41; 12:35; 13:21; 14:61; 15:32). The reader has known from the beginning (1:1) that Jesus is the Messiah. Peter becomes the first character in the narrative to speak the word *Messiah*. After the confession, Jesus states that the scribes misunderstand the identity of the Messiah (12:35). Jesus speaks as well of times to come when his followers are not to believe claims that the Messiah is here (13:21). The two final instances of the use of the word *Messiah* are the ironic recognition of Jesus by the High Priest (14:61) and the taunts of the chief priest and scribes (15:32).

- In addition, the preacher might look at other pericopae in which titles are attributed directly or indirectly to Jesus: Son of God (1:1; 3:11; 15:39), Beloved Son (1:11; 9:7; 12:6), Holy One of God (1:24), Son of the Most High God (5:7), King of the Jews (15:2, 9, 12, 18, 26), Son of the Blessed (14:61), Son of David (10:47–48; 12:35).

- It is significant to notice *who* in the narrative is speaking these various titles. To an extraordinary degree, these words are assigned to demons and to Jesus' enemies, characters with whom the implied reader is not likely to identify. What does it mean that Peter, the first of the disciples, is portrayed as saying the things that demons and enemies say?

- Peter is the first human character in the narrative to confess Jesus as "Messiah." Peter will later deny Jesus, saying, "I do not know this man" (14:71). Jesus has told the disciples that all who want to be his followers must "deny themselves" and be willing to lose their lives for the sake of Jesus (8:34–35). Peter denies Jesus to save his own life.

- Peter's answer begins, "You are." There are five passages in Mark in which Jesus is so addressed (1:11; 3:11; 8:29; 14:61; 15:2).

- In the immediate aftermath of the confession, Peter is rebuked (*epitimao*) by Jesus. This pattern is found elsewhere in Mark. A demon who calls Jesus "the Holy One of God" is rebuked (1:24–25). The unclean spirits who say to Jesus, "You are the Son of God" are rebuked (3:11–12).[9] What does it

---

[9] Bartimaeus calls Jesus "Son of David" and is rebuked not by Jesus, but by the crowd (10:47–48).

mean that Jesus responds to Peter in the same way he has responded to demons?

• Mark contains relatively few direct statements by Peter. Those statements that are quoted by the narrator can be examined (8:29; 9:5; 10:28; 11:21; 14:29, 71). Juxtaposing the first of these ("You are the Messiah") with the last ("I do not know this man you are talking about") presents an intriguing set of statements.

• Did Peter understand the meaning of his confession?[10] Jesus' three predictions of his passion (8:31; 9:31; 10:33–34) follow the confession. In each instance the disciples behave in ways that betray them; they do not understand what Jesus has said (8:32–33; 9:33–34; 10:35–41).

Exploring such connections with the gospel of Mark benefits the preacher. It offers a broader view of the pericope being studied, opening the preacher's eyes to the larger narrative. In the process, questions will arise that intrigue the preacher. It is not necessary that this process of brainstorming be exhaustive. Neither is it expected that preachers will be drawn into a detailed study of each passage that surfaces. I assume that each preacher will discover different connections with the larger story.

There are two hoped-for outcomes of this brainstorming. First, the preacher will identify a number of narrative threads running through Mark that surface in the pericope under consideration. The preacher will focus on *one* of these threads in crafting the sermon. Second, the preacher will ponder the questions that the narrative raises. It is through these questions that the narrative has the potential of speaking to the preacher in a new way.

Establishing the Sermon's Plotline

The sermon is integrated by its movement from tension to resolution, its homiletical plot. Looking at the material gathered, the preacher must develop the basic plotline of the sermon. Though there will be many questions that arise in the process of brainstorming, focus on one question. Does the sermon text *ask* the question or *answer* the question? If the text raises the question, where in the

---

[10]Juel observes, "His confession is not wrong…but there is more to confession than getting the words right…The right words are important, but they do not necessarily lead to life." See *A Master of Surprise,* 74–75.

larger narrative can a clue to resolution be found? If the text answers the question, where in the larger narrative is that question raised?

Disequilibrium. Peter's confession raises the question that my sermon will address: Did Peter get it right? I am choosing to use the text to pose the question and to find a source of resolution elsewhere in the Marcan narrative. I am intrigued by the reversal that takes place immediately following Peter's confession. The reader has known all along who Jesus is. The reader has watched the characters in the story struggle to understand who Jesus is. The reader has heard the questions they have raised. The reader has observed that the disciples have scarcely more insight than the public at large.

Finally, at 8:29, for the first time in the narrative, a human character voices the truth that the reader already knows. The reader wants to believe that the truth has finally broken in on Peter. Jesus' reply, however, fails to confirm the truth of Peter's confession. He *rebukes* Peter to silence, just as he has previously rebuked the demons to silence. Jesus goes on to describe what will happen to the Messiah…and is rebuked by Peter. Jesus rebukes Peter and calls him "Satan." The confession narrative invites the reader to wonder if Peter has understood who Jesus is, if Peter has "gotten it right." The sermon will exploit the way the Marcan narrative raises this question for its readers.

Resolution. The sermon will find its clue to resolution in the account of Peter's denial (14:66–72). This is the final scene in which Peter is physically present on Mark's narrative stage. Just hours before, Peter has stated emphatically that he will not desert Jesus, even if it means he must die with him (14:29–31). Now, in a time of crisis, Peter is challenged by a slave woman and then by a group of bystanders who make a series of three true assertions. Peter finds himself unable to affirm his association with Jesus (14:67–68) or his association with Jesus' followers (14:69–70). Instead, Peter "began to curse, and he swore an oath, 'I do not know this man you are talking about'" (14:71).

The denial pericope will provide a rephrasing of the sermon's question. Up to this point, the sermon will ask, Did Peter get it right? At the point of Peter's denial, the question becomes, What does it mean to get it right? To confess Jesus rightly involves more than correctly stating orthodox beliefs concerning his identity. It is a matter of affirming one's solidarity with Jesus and with Jesus' followers, especially in the time of crisis.

Being Open to Contemporary Images

Sometimes illustrative material will occur to the preacher in the course of brainstorming and will contribute to the sermon's conceptualization. At other times, illustrative material will emerge once the sermon's plotline is established. The two images below occurred to me once the sermon's plotline was clear.

- The homeless man. In the safe context of discussing social policy, it is easy to criticize policies that have led to the problem of homelessness. It is easy to say the right thing. However, encountering a homeless person on the street is a different matter. We all know what it is like to be confronted on the sidewalk by a homeless person asking us for money. We often choose to ignore the homeless person, passing by without eye contact.
- Reconciling Congregations. Epworth United Methodist Church, the congregation for which this sermon was written, is a reconciling congregation, which means it is one of a small number of United Methodist local churches that explicitly welcome gays and lesbians to be a part of their worshiping community. It is easy to celebrate openness in the safe environment of Epworth. I will wonder aloud how easy it would be in a more hostile context.

Weaving the Sermon

The sermon that follows weaves together a number of threads gathered in the process of brainstorming. The crafting of a sermon is a creative act, and there is no one "right" way to construct the message. The following is an example of *one* way to weave a sermon on the Marcan version of Peter's confession.

Let me reemphasize this point. I would never want to suggest that the sermon that follows is the only legitimate sermon that can be preached from Mark's telling of Peter's confession. Many appropriate sermons can arise from this text. I encourage the reader to engage in a conversation with the Marcan narrative, to find creative threads running through the larger story, and to address particular issues that are appropriate to the communities to which you proclaim the gospel. I hope to encourage imaginative wrestling with biblical texts. I expect that preachers will discover exciting and intriguing ways to preach from synoptic narratives, ways I could not have anticipated.

❖

Getting It Right
Mark 8:27–30

Did Peter get it right or wrong?
"You are the Messiah," he said,
and then Jesus *rebuked* them to tell no one about him.
A strange response.
We'd expect "You got it right" or "You got it wrong."
But a rebuke? What does that mean?
"Who do you say that I am?"
Peter said, "You are the Messiah."
And Jesus went on to say what "Messiah" meant.
It meant suffering. It meant rejection.
It meant that he would be killed.
It meant that he would rise again.
Peter never got past the word *suffering.*
He was horrified. Scandalized.
Peter *rebuked* Jesus.
And Jesus rebuked Peter and called him "Satan."
"You are the Messiah."
Did Peter get it right? Or was something wrong?

We know the word is correct.
Mark told us as much in the first sentence of his gospel.
"The beginning of the good news of Jesus the Messiah,
    the Son of God."
And the demons have known all along.
The demon in the synagogue at Nazareth said,
"I know who you are, the Holy One of God."
Jesus rebuked the demon.
Wherever Jesus traveled, the demons fell down before him.
"You are the Son of God," they said.
Jesus rebuked them.

There was one man possessed by so many demons that
he was made to live among the tombs.
"What have you to do with me,
   Jesus, Son of the Most High God?"
Jesus sent those demons into a herd of swine,
then watched the herd of 2,000 self-destruct
as it rushed down a steep bank
   and drowned in the sea below.
The demons got the words right,
but is getting the words right the point?
Is Mark making the demons an example for us?

Actually, lots of people in Mark's story get the words right.
The crowd by the side of the road on Palm Sunday
   hail Jesus as the "one who comes
   in the name of the Lord."
What would the crowd cry a few days later?
Out of the mouth of the high priest came the question,
"Are you the Messiah, the Son of the Blessed One?"
And when Jesus affirmed the words the priest had spoken,
what did the priest do next?
Pilate asked,
"Are you the King of the Jews?"
Though his question got it right,
what was the next action Pilate took?
The Roman soldiers got the words right too.
"Hail, King of the Jews!"
Did their actions honor Jesus as king?
What about the centurion who carried out Jesus' execution?
"Truly this man was a son of God."
He said the right words,
but how many sons of God
   had he put to death in his career?

Yes, lots of folks got it right—
demons, priests, politicians, soldiers—
even disciples.
Judas was one of the Twelve.
He made it into the inner circle,

then betrayed Jesus to death.
The twelve disciples got the words right.
They vowed to follow him to the very end.
What happened in the very end?
Every last one of them deserted.
Peter got the words right—
"You are the Messiah"—
but when crunch time came,
what did Peter do?

Jesus was on trial for his life inside the high priest's house.
Peter was outside in the courtyard.
One of the high priest's servant-girls stared at him.
She recognized him:
    "You were with Jesus, the man from Nazareth."
Peter denied it.
She began to tell the bystanders: "This man is one of *them*."
Peter denied it.
The bystanders picked up on Peter's accent:
"Certainly, you are one of them; for you are a Galilean."
Cursing and swearing, Peter denied it.
"I do not know this man you are talking about."
I am not with Jesus.
I am not one of them.
I do not know this man.

What does it mean to get it right?

It's one thing to speak the right words
    when it doesn't cost anything.
It's easy to say the right thing
    when we're just asked our opinion.
It's quite another thing to proclaim our convictions
    when they may make us unpopular.
It's quite another thing to take an action
    that strikes at the heart of our fears.
Yes, I am concerned for the homeless,
    if you ask my opinion,
        and I will decry the social policies

that have taken away the safety net
　　of the most vulnerable members of society,
even as tax loopholes for multibillion-dollar
　　multinational corporations are preserved.
But when I walk down Shattuck Avenue
　　and see him sitting up ahead,
I slowly drift to the other edge of the sidewalk
　　and suddenly take an interest in the store display.
I hear him speaking to me,
　　but I pretend that he is not even there.
I do not know this man.
Why am I so afraid?
Yes, I am proud to be associated with this church,
　　to be a part of a Reconciling Congregation.
And here in this pulpit, this is easy for me to say.
But if I found myself outside the safe environment
　　of Epworth, Berkeley, the Bay Area,
　　　　would I be so forthright?
Were I invited to preach in a conservative, rural church,
　　would I dare talk about
　　the Reconciling Congregation movement?
Would I dare identify myself as being from Berkeley,
　　supporting the rights of homosexuals in our society
　　　　and in the church?
Would I dare speak of the contradiction
　　of our denomination, which declares
　　"homosexuals…are individuals of sacred worth"
　　　　yet refuses to ordain gay men and lesbian women?
Would I dare say those things?
Or would I equivocate?
I am not one of them.
Why do I care about being popular?

By the end of Mark's gospel,
　　everyone who was supposed to do or say something
　　has left it undone or unspoken…out of fear.
Judas betrayed.
Disciples ran.
Peter denied.

The women said nothing.
The surroundings were hostile, and they were afraid.
It's left to us who read and hear Mark's story
to say and do what still needs to be done and said.
Can you imagine yourself
acknowledging the greeting of the man on the street corner
or the man on trial?
Yes, I do know this man.
And he may not be popular right now,
but I believe in what he says, and I believe in what he does.
Can you imagine yourself
sharing convictions that will make you unpopular?
Yes, I am one of *them.*
I support the Reconciling Movement.
And you may be offended by who we are,
by what we do,
by what we stand for,
but I *am* one of them.

When Jesus is inside, on trial for his life—
When you are outside,
   supporting him the best way you know how—
When someone stares at you
   and recognizes you as one of *them*—
When they challenge you:
   "You are with Jesus, the man from Nazareth."
When you answer, "Yes I am, and he's the Messiah"—
Isn't that what it means to get it right?

Reflection on the Sermon

Did Peter Get It Right or Wrong?

The sermon opens by using Peter's confession to upset the equilibrium, to raise the question that the sermon will address: Did Peter get it right or wrong? The opening exploits the ambiguity of the Marcan text. Jesus responds to Peter's confession with a rebuke. The sermon does not attempt to resolve the ambiguity, but uses it to amplify the question. I am taking the clue from Mark's own rhetoric by embracing, rather than resolving, the narrative's ambiguity.

The immediate aftermath of the text—the first passion prediction announcement—is briefly introduced. I mention Peter's rebuking of Jesus' word and Jesus' rebuking of Peter in order to heighten the opening question further. By rejecting the notion that the Messiah is to suffer, has Peter gotten it wrong? Closure is given to the opening by repeating a variation of the question with which it opened.

I have woven variations of the phrase "Did Peter get it right?" throughout the sermon. Variations include "the word is correct," "got the words right," "getting the words right," "right words," and "say the right thing." The repetition of this question helps unify the sermon.

We know the word is correct. The next section of the sermon uses two threads gathered in the process of brainstorming and researching the text. One thread is the inside knowledge that the reader possesses. Mark's readers know that the title used by Peter is correct. The information has been provided to the reader in the opening verse or title of the gospel (1:1). A second thread follows the demons' identifications of Jesus (1:23–26; 3:11–12; 5:1–13). Jesus rebukes or silences the demons who recognize him. By using this thread in the sermon, I link Jesus' response to Peter with his response to the demons. The demons, like Peter, have spoken the right words. But are the demons a paradigm of discipleship for Mark? The section concludes with two rhetorical questions to this effect. I hint that the answer will be no. However, I avoid making a clear statement in the indicative; this would answer the sermon's question and collapse the narrative tension too early.

Actually, lots of people in Mark's story get the words right. I introduce a third thread, the ironic recognition of Jesus by his enemies. The sermon relates the attribution of christological titles to Jesus by various characters in the story—the crowd at Palm Sunday (11:9–10), the high priest (14:61), Pilate (15:2), and the soldiers (15:18). Again, the sermon communicates the problematic nature of these "confessions" by asking the congregation to remember (as opposed to stating) the characters' behavior following the act of speaking correct words. The purpose of this rhetorical strategy is, again, to maintain a level of ambiguity and suspense in the sermon.

Yes, lots of folks got the words right—demons, priests, politicians, soldiers, even disciples. I weave in a fourth thread, the falling away of the disciples. This section of the sermon draws an inference from the text. If Peter spoke on behalf of the Twelve, it is reasonable to assume that the other eleven disciples—including Judas—attributed christological titles to Jesus as well. Mark has gone to great lengths to build up the disciples, then topple them in full view of the reader. The sermon exploits this feature of the narrative. I refer to the disciples' fate in the plot of Mark. Judas betrays Jesus, and the Twelve desert him despite unanimous vows to the contrary. I refer again to Peter's confession, the textual basis of the sermon, but maintain narrative tension by asking, "What did Peter do?" instead of referring directly to his denial.

Jesus was on trial for his life inside the high priest's house. This section of the sermon introduces the clue to resolution. I use the story of Peter's denial to transpose the sermon's question into a new form that incorporates a new emphasis. Instead of asking, "Did Peter get it right?" I begin to ask, "What does it mean to get it right?"

Even though the congregation knows what Peter did, I maintain a sense of anticipation by relating the denial in narrative form. I take four sentences to establish the setting in which the denial took place, a much slower narrative pace than is found in the rest of the sermon. Again, I am taking my clue from Mark's own rhetoric. The threefold form of the denial is maintained, but Peter's own words are withheld. I repeat the phrase "Peter denied it," allowing this use of repetition to make its own rhetorical impact. Having built up to a moment of crisis in the story and in the sermon, I finally quote Peter's own words: "I do not know this man you are talking about" (14:71). The purpose is to let the irony of this statement have its full effect upon the listeners. Finally, I summarize the content of Peter's denial: "*I* am not with Jesus. *I* am not one of them. *I* do not know this man." Peter does not deny Jesus' identity as Messiah or Son of God; his denial consists of disassociating himself from Jesus and his followers in a time of crisis. This is the sermon's clue to resolution.

It's one thing to speak the right words when it doesn't cost anything. I introduce the first illustrative thread at this point in the sermon, relating the material discussed above under the heading "the homeless man." I tie this thread into the fabric of the sermon by repeating the words of Peter's denial: "I do not know this man."

Yes, I am proud to be associated with this church, to be a part of a reconciling congregation. I introduce the second illustrative thread, discussed above under the heading "reconciling congregations." This thread is woven into the sermon by repeating a phrase from the section on Peter's denial: "I am not one of them."

By the end of Mark's gospel, everyone who was supposed to do or say something has left it undone or unspoken...out of fear. This section introduces the sermon's denouement. The thread of the falling away of the disciples is reintroduced here, as are the two illustrative threads, "the homeless man" and "reconciling congregations." Up until this point, the tone of the sermon has been somewhat negative. I now take a positive tone, asking the listeners to imagine themselves engaging in these new behaviors, to imagine themselves "getting it right."

When Jesus is inside, on trial for his life. The ending of the sermon puts the listener in Peter's place. The listener answers the accusation "You are with Jesus, the man from Nazareth" with a positive statement: "Yes I am, and he's the Messiah." The sermon closes with a rhetorical question: "Isn't that what it means to get it right?" This ending is a "loose thread" that permits the listener to draw her or his own conclusion.

Seen as a whole, this sermon attempts to interpret Peter's confession in light of the entire Marcan narrative. Mark introduces ambiguity into the text in the immediate aftermath of the confession, allowing the reader to question in what way Peter's response may be deficient. By juxtaposing the confession pericope with the story of the denial, this sermon represents *one way* in which the reader/listener may resolve that ambiguity. Since the Marcan confession is preached every three years, it is anticipated that the preacher's imagination will lead him or her to explore multiple approaches over the course of a pastorate.

3

Reading and Preaching
Luke–Acts

As I suggested with the chapter on the gospel of Mark, there are a number of ways in which this chapter may be used. Specifically, it provides the reading of Luke–Acts from which I wrote a sermon on the Lucan version of Peter's confession. More generally, this material offers the preacher a brief overview of the narrative world projected by Luke–Acts. It can be useful whenever we preach from, or lead Bible studies on, the gospel of Luke and the Acts of the Apostles.

Reading Luke–Acts

Why Luke–Acts? The canonizers certainly did not encourage readers to approach Luke–Acts as a single narrative; they interrupted its continuity with the gospel of John. Realize, however, that their decision represents an act of interpretation. We are free—dare I say obligated—to interpret scripture responsibly for ourselves. There is substantial evidence that Luke and Acts are intended to be read as a single narrative. Acts, at the very least, is the continuation of the story begun in the gospel of Luke. Luke is addressed to an "inscribed reader" named Theophilus[1] (Lk. 1:3) and ends with an

---

[1]Who is Theophilus? Is he a Roman official to whom Luke is addressing this chronicle, hoping to win official favor for the Christian movement? Is Theophilus Luke's benefactor,

account of Jesus' ascension (Lk. 24:50–53). Acts, also inscribed to Theophilus (Acts 1:3), begins by referring to "the first book…[in which] I wrote about all that Jesus did and taught from the beginning until the day when he was taken up to heaven" (Acts 1:1–2). The first event narrated in Acts is a reprise of the ascension story found at the conclusion of Luke (Acts 1:6–11).

Based on this evidence, I have made the interpretive decision to undertake a reading of Luke–Acts as the story-as-a-whole. I will pursue a number of issues as they are developed through the whole of Luke's narrative.

(1) *Controversy in Luke–Acts.* The controversy *behind* this narrative is the issue that led to the church's first great crisis: the relationship of Jewish Christians and Gentile Christians in the church. This controversy becomes explicit at two places in Luke–Acts, Acts 11 and 15.

(2) *Conflict within the narrative.* The conflict *within* the narrative concerns the assertion that God's salvation is intended not only for Jews but for all the nations of the earth.

(3) *The pious and observant adherents of Jesus.* Jesus and the figures in the narrative sympathetic to Jesus are characterized as pious Jews who are well thought of by all the people. They are found frequently in the temple, are faithful in prayer, and are active in fellowship.

(4) *The pivotal role of Peter in Luke–Acts.* While Jesus is the major character in Luke, and Paul the major character at the end of Acts, Peter plays the pivotal role in the narrative-as-a-whole. His transformation in the narrative models the transformation Luke hopes to effect in the implied reader.

Controversy in Luke–Acts

In a murder mystery, the clue that solves the crime often turns out to be a small detail overlooked by the casual observer. While the blunt evidence of the crime stares all observers in the face, the perceptive detective notices apparently insignificant clues—ordinary things that would be of no importance save for the fact that they

---

providing the funding that enabled Luke to complete this substantial literary work? Are these books simply directed to "friends of God," a literal translation of *Theo* (God) *philos* (friend)? Ultimately, these are historical questions that we will suspend in order to approach Luke–Acts as a narrative world.

seem out of place. The same can be said for interpreting any narrative. The reader must of course take into account the major events in the story, but the best clues to the narrative's meaning may consist of what the reader does *not* expect to find.

Luke–Acts is an epic drama, formally addressed to an individual referred to as "most excellent Theophilus." The narrative begins before the birth of Jesus and tells of his life, childhood, ministry, death, resurrection, and ascension. It tells of the church's empowerment, of an apostolic witness that heals the sick, raises the dead, and wins thousands of converts. It chronicles how the gospel is taken into Judea, Samaria, and to the ends of the Earth. It ends with Paul proclaiming the gospel in the seat of Roman power, at the political center of the *pax romana*.

Yet set within the scope of this epic narrative are "minutes" of two church meetings (Acts 11:1–18; 15:1–35; 21:25). Why is seemingly banal material found in the midst of such an extraordinary drama? I ask preachers to ponder this fact in light of our own experiences in the local church. Our churches occasionally face important but controversial decisions. Votes may be taken on issues around which no consensus has emerged, leaving winners and losers, hard feelings, and a divided church. There can be dissension for years over what was argued, who said what to whom, what decision was actually reached, and why. Proponents of both sides continue to tell their stories of that decision. Of course, those tellings of the story may differ dramatically.

The two meetings reported by Luke–Acts deal with the church's first great crisis. As the gospel spread from Jerusalem and Judea into Samaria and to the ends of the Earth, Gentiles began to hear the good news and became part of the Christian movement. They came to the church with religious backgrounds quite different from those of Jewish Christians. The practices of the new Gentile Christian congregations were likewise different from those of Jewish Christian "old-timers." The church was facing the problem of a cultural divide that would prove quite difficult to bridge.

Were Gentile converts to Christianity obligated to become observant Jews? Did they have to keep the kosher dietary laws? Must male converts undergo the ritual of circumcision? Were Jewish Christians meant to have fellowship with Gentile believers? Were they called to overcome their cultural and religious aversion to associating with Gentiles? These issues related directly to the identity of the growing Christian movement and had important implications for the success of its future mission. Paul's letters, written in the '50s and '60s, struggled theologically and exegetically with these questions. The fact that Luke–Acts is still addressing them in the '80s or '90s suggests that the issues were not neatly resolved.[2]

Far from being an extraneous detail, these apparently out-of-place church minutes are the very point of Luke's story. I am arguing that Luke–Acts has been written *in response* to the issue addressed at these meetings. The very call to take the gospel "to the ends of the earth" is at stake. How is the church to understand the relationship of Jewish and Gentile Christians in its midst? What are the implications for the church's faith and practice? In Luke's account, the meeting has a clear outcome. Gentiles are *not* obligated to keep the law. Kosher food laws are *not* an excuse for Jewish Christians to decline table fellowship with Gentile Christians. Luke–Acts calls for a fully inclusive church; anything less puts needless fetters on the church's missional imperative. The implied author has structured the narrative to provide theological justification for this word to the church.

Homiletical reflection. We sometimes hear the notion that the "early church" was an idealized community of committed believers; they were so in tune with the Spirit that they were not stymied by the kinds of conflicts that trouble the church today. Luke does contribute to that notion by some of his characterizations of the early church: They shared all things in common, spent much time in the temple, attended to the apostles' teaching, and were constant in prayer. However, a careful reading of the whole of Acts cannot support such a notion. It reveals that sometimes members of the early church failed to live out their faith with integrity (e.g., Ananias and Sapphira). It reveals considerable controversy about how to interpret the Bible in a new context (the relevance of the Torah for Gentile converts). It reveals that some members, though sincere and fervent in their own

---

[2] The way Luke's story relates the "minutes" of one meeting is not identical with the way others told the story. Compare Acts 15 with Paul's account written a generation earlier (Gal. 2:1–10). Peter's role seems much more equivocal in Paul's version. Compare Luke's position on the significance of the law with the teaching of Matthew's Jesus in a roughly contemporaneous narrative (Mt. 5:17–20). Does the Matthean Jesus command the disciples to teach all nations (literally, "all Gentiles") to obey the law as Matthew's Jesus so authoritatively interprets it (Mt. 28:19–20)?

beliefs, were insensitive to the feelings and needs of other members of the church. It reveals that Christians had to recognize and confront their own prejudices in order that God's purposes not be impeded. It reveals that church communities honestly tried to resolve problems and find common ground, only to have the problems resurface and the common ground disappear. It reveals a human tendency to demonize those with whom one passionately disagrees.

Pastors will recognize these same traits in our own congregations and denominations today. It is not an easy thing to live in community, to share one's faith with both passion and sensitivity, to reach consensus on difficult issues, to love those with whom we disagree. This is perhaps the single most difficult and stressful dimension of pastoral leadership. Like it or not, one of our most important tasks as pastors is to manage conflict within the communities we serve. Churches facing conflict often choose the path of avoidance (not dealing with those issues about which there is disagreement) or confrontation (each side seeks to impose its will on the other). Collaboration (the search for a win–win solution) is the better path. Collaboration requires taking seriously the objectives of the person with whom one is in conflict, searching together for common goals, and finding ways of accomplishing those goals. James offers an example of a leader who tried to resolve conflict through collaboration; I will discuss James's role in the Jerusalem Conference in the next section.

There is a relationship between our efforts at conflict management and the rhetorical form that our preaching takes. If a pastor's efforts at conflict management are to be taken seriously, our rhetoric should model a collaborative style. Preaching should not avoid conflict, but engage real issues. Sermons will thus deal with subject matter over which there is genuine disagreement. However, such issues should not be dealt with in a confrontational manner that advocates one's own position and seeks to demolish the position the other side is taking. Rather, if sermons deal honestly and respectfully with opposing viewpoints, preachers are modeling collaboration. To be specific, an opposing viewpoint should be portrayed in a way that the proponents of that position would recognize as being a fair representation of their views. Through a collaborative rhetorical style, a preacher embodies how Christians are to deal with one another when they disagree.

Conflict within the Narrative

The numerous instances of conflict within Luke-Acts can be read in light of this overarching theory of the controversy addressed by the narrative. The church of Luke's day was struggling with a difficult and painful cultural divide. The church's mission necessitated that this divide be bridged, but many of the characters in Luke–Acts, both Jews and Jewish Christians, find the prospect troubling and even offensive. Their offense finds explicit expression at numerous points in Luke–Acts.

Hints of conflict in the birth narrative. Conflict is introduced in the birth narrative. At first, it is simply hinted at in the speeches of various characters in the prologue. Gabriel's announcement to Zechariah speaks of the ultimate purpose of his yet-to-be-born son's ministry: "to make ready a people prepared for the Lord" (Lk. 1:17). Who are included among this "people" to be made ready? Mary's song (the Magnificat) declares that God's mercy will bring about a great reversal. The proud, the powerful, and the rich will be brought down. God's mercy will be experienced by "those who fear him," the lowly, and the hungry (Lk. 1:51–53). Just who are those "lowly" who are to receive God's favor? Zechariah's prophecy declares that this inbreaking of mercy is "to give light to those who sit in darkness" (Lk. 1:79). Who are "those who sit in darkness"? The angels who announce good news to the shepherds sing of "great joy for all the people" (Lk. 2:10). Does "all" the people really mean what it says?

Notice the narrative artistry with which Luke finally makes the conflict explicit. Luke portrays an elderly man named Simeon, characterized as "righteous and devout," who is guided by the Spirit to come to the temple. Simeon encounters the holy family present for Jesus' circumcision. As Simeon cradles the infant Jesus in his arms, he declares, "My eyes have seen your salvation, which you have prepared in the presence of all peoples, *a light for revelation to the Gentiles* and for glory to your people Israel" (Lk. 2:30–32, emphasis added). It is deeply ironic that the announcement of good news for the Gentiles is first made explicit on the occasion of a circumcision ritual. Circumcision was the sign of the covenant that heretofore had distinguished Jews from Gentiles.

The Lucan genealogy (Lk. 3:23–38) will make essentially the same point. While Matthew traced Jesus' ancestry back to Abraham, the patriarch of Israel, Luke will trace his ancestry to Adam, the progenitor of the entire human family. The scope of the salvation to come is universal. "All people" includes Gentiles.

Realized conflict in Nazareth. The idea that God is reaching out to Gentiles provokes a consistent response from some of the characters in Luke–Acts. The congregants in the synagogue at Nazareth are favorably impressed by Jesus' message until he mentions that Elijah was sent not to the widows of Israel but to "a widow at Zarephath in Sidon" during a time of famine. Jesus continues with a second and even more pointed illustration: Elisha did not cleanse the lepers of Israel, only Naaman the Syrian. The notion that God would show favor to Gentiles and not to Jews provokes anger. Jesus' listeners attempt to hurl him off a cliff (Lk. 4:25–29), foreshadowing the violence of the crucifixion at the climax of Luke's gospel and the stoning of Stephen in Acts.

Controversy in parables. It is notable that Luke's narrative includes a parable affirming that a Samaritan, rather than the priest or Levite, is the one who proves to be our neighbor (Lk. 10:25–37). The parable of the prodigal son (Lk. 15:11–32) ends with the younger brother inside the father's house at a great feast of celebration. He has been employed feeding pigs and so is ritually unclean. The older brother refuses to come in to celebrate the return of the lost brother. He refuses even to acknowledge the prodigal as his brother, referring to him as "this son of yours."[3] The older brother, like the worshipers in the synagogue at Nazareth, represents the implied reader of Luke's narrative, Jewish Christians who are resisting association with Gentile Christians within the church. The father represents the viewpoint of the implied author. He pleads with his older son to accept the long-lost prodigal as his brother.

Hints of conflict in the early chapters of Acts. The Acts of the Apostles begins, as the gospel of Luke has ended, with the call of the risen Jesus to the disciples:

> Thus it is written, that the Messiah is to suffer and to rise
> from the dead on the third day, and that repentance and

---

[3] John R. Donahue, *The Gospel in Parable: Metaphor, Narrative, and Theology in the Synoptic Gospels* (Philadelphia: Fortress Press, 1988), 157.

forgiveness of sins is to be proclaimed in his name *to all the Gentiles,* beginning from Jerusalem. (Lk. 24:46–47, author trans.)

You will be my witnesses in Jerusalem, in all Judea and Samaria, and to the ends of the earth. (Acts 1:8)

This missionary imperative sets up the plot and establishes the conflict of Acts.

Acts employs the same rhetorical strategy as did the gospel of Luke. The precise scope of God's promise of salvation is subtly introduced to the reader. Only hinted at at first, Luke eventually makes it explicit that the Gentiles are to be recipients of God's mercy. Peter's Pentecost sermon is addressed to "devout Jews from every nation under heaven." Peter tells them, "the promise is for you, for your children, and for all who are far away, everyone whom the Lord our God calls to him" (Acts 2:5, 39).[4] Who are the "far away"? Who is it that the Lord calls?

The "hints" continue. After healing a crippled beggar lying at the gate of the temple, Peter's sermon resumes a narrative thread first found in the Magnificat, God's promise to Abraham. Peter declares, "By means of your seed, *all the families of the earth* shall be blessed" (Acts 3:25, author trans.). Later, speaking to the council, Peter affirms that God has given the Holy Spirit "to those who obey him" (Acts 5:32). The speech enrages Peter's listeners, leaving the reader to wonder *why* this statement should have been so provocative to Peter's audience. The council members seem to know intuitively what the naïve reader of Acts has not yet learned.

Realized conflict in Acts. Throughout the first six chapters of Acts, the conflict has provoked strong emotional responses to the sermons of Peter and to the activities of the disciples. Physical violence erupts in Acts 7 when those who hear Stephen's sermon stone him to death. The stoning of Stephen initiates a "severe persecution…

---

[4] "The promise is…for all who are far away." The Greek word *makran,* an adverb translated "far away" or "far off," is the same word used in the parable of the prodigal son. "But while [the younger son] was still *far off,* his father saw him and was filled with compassion; he ran and put his arms around him and kissed him" (Lk. 15:20, emphasis added). Toward the end of Acts, Luke explicitly identifies those who are far away as the Gentiles. The final sentence in Paul's speech in his defense reports Jesus' words to him: "Go, for I will send you far away [*makran*] to the Gentiles" (Acts 22:21). This statement provokes calls from the crowd for Paul's death.

against the church in Jerusalem." This persecution becomes a turning point in the story. While the apostles remain in Jerusalem, the rest of the church departs, scattering into Judea and Samaria. Thus begins the outward movement of the gospel from Jerusalem to the ends of the earth.

Just as Jesus became the focus of conflict in Luke, Paul becomes the ultimate lightning rod for conflict in Acts.[5] Following his conversion in Acts 9, Paul begins his ministry of proclaiming Jesus. It is a ministry of continuous conflict. He debates his theological opponents in many venues, often inciting his listeners in the process. Consider Paul's sermon to the Jews of Antioch:

> It was necessary that the word of God should be spoken first to you [the Jews]. Since you reject it and judge yourselves to be unworthy of eternal life, we are now turning to the Gentiles. For so the Lord has commanded us, saying, "I have set you to be a light for the Gentiles, so that you may bring salvation to the ends of the earth." (Acts 13:46–47)

Notice that the theme introduced in Zechariah's prayer (Lk. 1:79, "to give light to those who sit in darkness") and made explicit by Simeon (Lk. 2:32, "a light for revelation to the Gentiles") has now come to narrative fruition. The different groups in Paul's audience respond to the sermon quite differently. On the one hand, the Gentiles were glad to hear this word and many became believers (Acts 13:48). On the other hand, the Jews incited the leading men and women of the city and stirred up persecution against Paul (Acts 13:50). What has so angered the latter group? Paul made the offensive claim that God's salvation is inclusive. He asserts this offensive notion by quoting scripture (Isa. 42:6; 49:6), a fact that infuriates his audience.

---

[5]Notice the parallels between the beginning of the ministries of Jesus and Paul. After Jesus is baptized and filled with the Spirit (Lk. 3:21–22), he begins his ministry teaching in the synagogues (Lk. 4:14). Those who hear him are amazed and ask, "Is not this Joseph's son?" (Lk. 4:22). His listeners become enraged by his sermon and attempt to kill him, but Jesus passes through their midst and goes on his way (Lk. 4:29–30). Like Jesus, Paul's ministry begins after he has been baptized and filled with the Spirit (Acts 9:17–18). Paul begins his ministry by teaching in the synagogues, and those who hear him are amazed and ask, "Is not this the man who made havoc in Jerusalem?" His listeners plot to kill him, but Paul escapes in a basket through an opening in the wall (Acts 9:20–25). See Robert Tannehill, *The Narrative Unity of Luke–Acts: A Literary Interpretation,* vol. 2 (Minneapolis: Fortress Press, 1990), for his discussion of narrative parallels between the careers of Jesus and Paul.

Paul faces numerous threats throughout the rest of Acts. There are multiple attempts to kill him. He is stoned, arrested on several occasions, flogged, imprisoned with his feet in stocks, and persecuted. Ultimately, Paul travels to Jerusalem, where he is arrested, paralleling the events experienced by Jesus in the gospel.

Conflict within the Christian family. In the preceding material, Luke has characterized *some* of the Jews in the story as acting out of an instinctive aversion to Gentiles. The idea that God would bring salvation to all people, both Jews and Gentiles, is anathema to these characters. They respond with anger and sometimes physical violence.

Luke's concern, however, is to address the conflict that continues to disrupt the Christian family, the conflict to which his readers are parties. Explicit conflict *within* the Christian family surfaces in the narrative after the conversion of Cornelius and his household. As Peter was preaching, "the Holy Spirit fell upon all who heard the word. The circumcised believers who had come with Peter were astounded that the gift of the Holy Spirit had been poured out even on the Gentiles" (Acts 10:44–45). Observing the gift of the Spirit on the Gentile believers, Peter orders the baptism of the first Gentile converts.

Word that Gentiles had become believers reaches the church in Jerusalem. This news creates consternation. When Peter returns to Jerusalem, he is criticized for having shared table fellowship with Gentiles. "The circumcised believers criticized [Peter], saying, 'Why did you go to uncircumcised men and eat with them?'" (Acts 11:2–3). Peter responds by telling of his vision and of the voice that spoke three times from heaven: "What God has made clean, you must not call profane" (Acts 10:15; 11:9). These words abrogate the law's dietary restrictions. Peter further asserts the Spirit's direction "not to make a distinction between them and us" (Acts 11:12). Peter's critics are silenced by these words and give praise that "God has given even to the Gentiles the repentance that leads to life" (Acts 11:18).

The conflict is far from resolved, however, and comes to a head in the fifteenth chapter of Acts. The setting is Antioch, where Paul has enjoyed a fruitful ministry. "Then certain individuals came down from Judea and were teaching the brothers, 'Unless you are circumcised according to the custom of Moses, you cannot be saved'" (Acts 15:1). Paul debates the matter with these individuals, then goes to Jerusalem to discuss the question with "the apostles and the elders."

In this episode, the opposing position is stated first. "Some believers who belonged to the sect of the Pharisees stood up and said, 'It is necessary for them to be circumcised and ordered to keep the law of Moses'" (Acts 15:5). Peter states the opposing argument. He cites the action of God by which he was chosen to "be the one through whom the Gentiles would hear the message of the good news and become believers" (Acts 15:7). He recalls the gift of the Holy Spirit to the Gentiles and reemphasizes that God "has made no distinction between them and us" (Acts 15:9). Peter responds to the argument about the necessity of circumcision and obedience to the Mosaic law by making three points. First, such a position puts God to the test. Second, it burdens the Gentiles with an unbearable yoke. Third, it denies that both Jews and Gentiles "will be saved through the grace of the Lord Jesus" (Acts 15:10–11).

James is characterized as the mediator. He acknowledges the positions taken by Paul and Peter. He interprets this pouring out of God's favor on the Gentiles as a fulfillment of the prophets. He draws the conclusion that Gentile believers should not be troubled with the whole of the Mosaic law. At the same time, he recognizes the concerns of the Pharisaic believers, proposing that the Gentiles abstain only from a number of particularly abhorrent practices: "from things polluted by idols and from fornication and from whatever has been strangled and from blood" (Acts 15:20).

James's compromise proposal carries the day. A letter containing his language is conveyed to "believers of Gentile origin" by Paul, Barnabas, and two leaders from the Jerusalem church. Luke characterizes the Gentile recipients as accepting this decision with joy (Acts 15:31).

Although the conflict appears to have been resolved by the Jerusalem Conference, the issue simply will not go away. When Paul returns to Jerusalem in Acts 21, James and the elders report to him rumors being circulated among Jewish Christians.

> You see, brother, how many thousands of believers there are among the Jews, and they are all zealous for the law. They have been told about you that you teach all the Jews living among the Gentiles to forsake Moses, and that you tell them not to circumcise their children or observe the customs. (Acts 21:20–21)

The elders propose that Paul participate in a rite of purification to demonstrate that these rumors are groundless. Paul's participation will show that he observes and guards the law. Paul takes their recommendation and submits to the rite. This action has unintended consequences. He is seen in the temple by "the Jews from Asia" who repeat the rumors in even more extreme language: "This is the man who is teaching everyone everywhere against our people, our law, and this place." They make the false accusation that Paul "has actually brought Greeks into the temple and has defiled this holy place" (Acts 21:28). After the ensuing riot, Paul defends himself, quoting at the conclusion of his sermon Jesus' words to him on the Damascus Road: "Go, for I will send you far away to the Gentiles." This statement provokes a harsh rejoinder from the crowd: "Away with such a fellow from the earth! For he should not be allowed to live" (Acts 22:21–22). The scene sets up Paul's arrest and his final journey to stand trial in Rome.

From the beginning of the birth narrative until Paul's arrest in Jerusalem, Luke–Acts has addressed a concern demonstrated consistently by a group of Jews and Jewish Christians. The influx of Gentiles into the church has breached traditional boundaries between Jews and Gentiles. Jews, heretofore, have been distinguished from Gentiles by the rite of circumcision and by their observance of the Mosaic law. They have remained ritually pure by avoiding unkosher food and table fellowship with Gentiles. The events of Acts—Peter's vision, the conversion of Cornelius, the Jerusalem Conference—have changed all this. The message of Luke–Acts is that God makes no distinction between Jews and Gentiles. All foods are declared to be clean. Peter is directed to accept the hospitality of Cornelius, a Gentile. Circumcision is deemed to be unnecessary for salvation. Jews are not to separate themselves from Gentiles anymore; they are to see themselves as "a light for the Gentiles."

Homiletical reflections. Our world has grown smaller in many ways. Air travel makes transportation quick if not exactly pleasant. E-mail enables people anywhere on earth to communicate with each other instantaneously and practically cost-free, if they are connected to the Internet. The global economy makes the economies of the world interdependent. We no longer live in the homogeneous small-town settings that our grandparents took for granted. We live in a world in which many cultures, religions, and languages coexist. This creates a challenging context for our ministry and preaching, one not unlike that faced by the Jewish Christians we encounter in Luke–Acts. They moved through the Roman Empire faithful to Jesus' call to "be my witnesses…to the ends of the earth" (Acts 1:8). They were successful in their mission, but their very success brought about a new set of problems. Their witness brought them into contact with persons of many different cultural backgrounds, socioeconomic conditions, and religious traditions. As the church experienced growth, its membership became diverse. The life of a diverse community posed thorny challenges.

Church growth research indicates that growing churches tend to be homogeneous. Researchers do not necessarily endorse the theological implications of a church's targeting a specific population in planning its program. They are simply reporting the data gained by their studies: Churches that promote and celebrate the diversity of their membership tend to have a harder time growing. Given human nature, it is easier to build large churches by attracting a community of similar people.

Luke–Acts compels us to reconsider the theological implications of church growth strategy. Pursuing growth through homogeneity may produce numerical success, but such success comes at a great price. The current crisis around the issue of homosexuality threatens the unity of many denominations and reveals a painful theological divide within the larger church. We seem incapable of addressing the problem, or even of hearing one another. I would argue that the problem begins in the local church. We tend to participate in local churches whose pastors and members share views similar to our own. When we join in Bible study or discussion groups, we tend not to hear the other view stated articulately and with integrity. We are not presented with opportunities to learn how to listen to those who disagree with us. We do not learn how to speak with one another about difficult issues. Rather, our own views are reinforced. It is all too easy to demonize the "other side" when it is not represented by a flesh-and-blood brother or sister we know and love.

The Jerusalem Conference represented an attempt by the larger church to mediate a dispute between Christians who held very different views on the role of the Torah in Christianity. The outcome of the narrative suggests that the resolution was not fabulously successful, perhaps because people in the local church needed to be involved in doing the work of finding common ground. If we never get the opportunity in our local churches to learn how to listen to and speak with those with whom we disagree, is it any wonder that we cannot resolve our problems in local judicatories, denominational assemblies, or ecumenical organizations?

The local church ought to be the junction where serious theological discussion begins. Such opportunities are sadly lacking in homogeneous local churches. We see the terrible consequences in Luke–Acts as Paul is arrested in Jerusalem because of fellow believers who distrusted and demonized him. We see the terrible consequences as today's churches face the pain of potential schism.

The Pious and Observant Adherents of Jesus

The preceding discussion has characterized Luke's narrative antagonists—Jews and Jewish Christians who have difficulty accepting that the scope of God's salvation includes Gentiles. Their opposition is a consistent feature of the narrative, from Jesus' sermon in the synagogue at Nazareth until the end of Acts. Luke's protagonists, on the other hand, embody the values Luke wishes to commend to his reader.

Characters in the prologue. What characterizes the protagonists and those allied with them? It may be surprising to notice that, from the beginning of the narrative, they are portrayed as *pious, observant Jews.*[6] Consider the cast of the prologue:

- Zechariah was a priest, and his wife Elizabeth was a descendent of Aaron, a daughter of a priestly family. The narrator describes both as "righteous before God, living blamelessly according to all the commandments and regulations of the Lord" (Lk. 1:6).
- Jesus' family is shown to be observant by their actions in the days following Jesus' birth. First, Jesus is circumcised on the eighth day. Second, Mary observes the rite of purification "according to the law of Moses." Third, they present their first-born to the Lord "as it is written in the law of the Lord."

---

[6]Donald Juel, *Luke-Acts: The Promise of History* (Atlanta: John Knox Press, 1983), 103–9.

Fourth, they offered the sacrifice that was "stated in the law of the Lord" (Lk. 2:22–24). Their visit to Jerusalem concludes with the narrator's comment that they "*fulfilled* everything required by the law of the Lord" before returning to Nazareth (Lk. 2:39, author trans.).

- Simeon is described by the narrator as "righteous and devout," with the Holy Spirit resting on him (Lk. 2:25).
- Anna is characterized as extremely devout. "She never left the temple but worshiped there with fasting and prayer night and day" (Lk. 2:37).

Characters in the main narrative. The characters aligned with Jesus in Luke and with Peter and Paul in Acts are variously described as righteous, God-fearing, devout, good, and full of the Spirit. Consider the portrayal of the following minor characters in Luke–Acts:

- Joseph of Arimathea was a member of the council that brought Jesus before Pilate. He is described as "a good and righteous man, who…had not agreed to their plan and action." We are told that "he was waiting expectantly for the kingdom of God" (Lk. 23:50–51). Joseph took care that Jesus was properly buried.
- The women who had come with Jesus from Galilee made preparations to anoint Jesus' body with spices and ointments. But "on the sabbath they rested according to the commandment" (Lk. 23:56).
- Luke portrays the large assembly that had come to Jerusalem for Pentecost as "devout" (Acts 2:5). After hearing Peter's sermon, three thousand of this assembly welcomed Peter's message and were baptized.
- Seven deacons were chosen to serve the Hellenist community in Jerusalem. They are presented as "men of good standing, full of the Spirit and of wisdom" (Acts 6:3).
- Stephen, one of the seven, is portrayed as "a man full of faith and the Holy Spirit" (Acts 6:5), "full of grace and power" (Acts 6:8), and "filled with the Holy Spirit" (Acts 7:55).
- Just as the narrator provided a positive characterization of Joseph of Arimathea, who buried Jesus, he praises the individuals who buried the martyred Stephen. They are presented as "devout men" (Acts 8:2).

- Cornelius, the first Gentile convert, is characterized as "a devout man who feared God," who "gave alms generously to the people and prayed constantly to God" (Acts 10:2). He is further described as "a righteous and God-fearing man who is well spoken of by the whole Jewish nation" (Acts 10:22, author trans.).
- Barnabas, Paul's fellow worker, is portrayed as "a good man, full of the Holy Spirit and of faith" (Acts 11:24).
- Ananias is presented as "a devout man according to the law and well spoken of by all the Jews living there" (Acts 22:12).
- Finally, we should notice the pious characterization of the Christian community at the end of Luke and in the early chapters of Acts. After Jesus' ascension, the eleven are described as "continually in the temple blessing God" (Lk. 24:53). This notation is repeated at the beginning of Acts: "All these were constantly devoting themselves to prayer, together with certain women, including Mary the mother of Jesus, as well as his brothers" (Acts 1:14). Following Pentecost, the believers "devoted themselves to the apostles' teaching and fellowship, to the breaking of bread and the prayers" (Acts 2:42). They practiced almsgiving and centered their lives around prayer in the temple and breaking bread at home. "All who believed were together and had all things in common; they would sell their possessions and goods and distribute the proceeds to all, as any had need. Day by day, as they spent much time together in the temple, they broke bread at home and ate their food with glad and generous hearts, praising God and having the goodwill of all the people" (Acts 2:44–47).

As the Jerusalem phase of Acts draws to a close, this note is repeated: "And every day in the temple and at home they did not cease to teach and proclaim Jesus as the Messiah" (Acts 5:42).

Homiletical reflections. Prayer plays an important role in Luke–Acts. Luke portrays Jesus and his adherents as pious, observant Jews. In addition, prayer sets the context for many of the crucial moments in the story.[7] The Lucan parable of the Pharisee and the tax collector (Lk. 18:9–14) broadens our understanding of the role of prayer

---

[7]For a brief summary of those moments and the role of prayer in Luke–Acts, see Donahue, *The Gospel in Parables*, 191–92.

in Luke–Acts. Consider the characterization of the Pharisee. He faithfully observes all the traditional forms of piety. He avoids immoral behavior, fasts, tithes, prays, and is well regarded because of his piety. The tax collector, by contrast, is characterized as someone who is regarded with contempt (*exoutheneo*) by the Pharisee and, by implication, by the implied reader.[8] Tax collecting "was one of the occupations forbidden to Jews. Tax collectors were ritually impure through contact with Gentiles at forbidden times, generally thought to be dishonest, and hardly popular in a country suffering economic exploitation through widespread taxation."[9] The tax collector, then, is one of many characters in Luke–Acts to whom the implied reader would feel instinctive aversion. Yet he provides a model of prayer.

Luke sets tax collectors and pharisees in tension throughout his narrative. While tax collectors came to John to be baptized, pharisees refused his baptism (Lk. 3:12; 7:30). Both times that Jesus eats with tax collectors, he is criticized for keeping this company (Lk. 5:30; 19:7). Perhaps most significant is the context of Luke 15. While "tax collectors and sinners" comprise the audience for the parables of the lost sheep, the lost coin, and the lost son, the pharisees and scribes grumble that Jesus would welcome and eat with such folk (Lk. 15:1–2). This contrast surfaces for us two observations about the place of prayer and piety in the Christian life.

First, true prayer adopts a posture of repentance rather than self-congratulation. The pharisee's prayer caricatures the self-congratulatory prayer of someone who possesses and enjoys stature within the religious community: "God, I thank you that I am not like other people…" (Lk. 18:11). By contrast, the tax collector possesses little honor in the eyes of the community. He remains "far off," not daring to approach the holy space in the area of the altar.[10] Even his posture is one of shame; he gazes downward, unable even to face heaven, beating his breast in remorse. His words are anything but self-congratulatory: "God, be merciful to me, a sinner!" (Lk. 18:13).

---

[8]Ironically, the only other character in Luke-Acts who is regarded with contempt (*exoutheneo*) is Jesus (Lk. 23:11; Acts 4:11).

[9]Donahue, *The Gospel in Parables*, 187–88.

[10]Like the prodigal son, the tax collector in his moment of repentance is characterized as being "far off" (*makran*). Luke makes explicit that God's promise is not just for pious Jews but for "all who are far away" (*makran*) (Acts 2:39).

Second, true prayer is consistent with an attitude of reaching out and welcoming others into fellowship, especially those for whom we feel disapproval. Prayer is inconsistent with an attitude of condemnation and exclusion. Prayer that brings about communion with God promotes love for one's neighbor. Prayer enables dialogue and engenders human intimacy. If in our practice of religion we feel justified in insulating ourselves from contact with our neighbors, saints and sinners alike, have we truly prayed?

The Pivotal Role of Peter in Luke–Acts

Luke characterizes Peter and the disciples in a far more positive fashion than did Mark. The *Marcan* disciples were hopelessly obtuse; each one denied, betrayed, or deserted Jesus, and none witnessed Jesus' crucifixion or resurrection. Luke offers a more optimistic view of the disciples. They, along with the women, watch the crucifixion from a distance (Lk. 23:49; cf. Mk. 15:58–59). The Lucan disciples encounter, recognize, and are spoken to by the risen Christ. They are instrumental in the continuing mission in the Acts of the Apostles. The ending of the gospel of Luke leaves the reader with the image of the disciples as a tight-knit community of joyful worshipers (Lk. 24:52–53), a characterization that is repeated in the opening chapters of Acts (Acts 2:44–47).

Peter is the pivotal character in Luke–Acts. He is characterized as an attractive figure with whom the implied reader can easily identify. Peter's transformation in the course of the narrative models the transformation that the implied reader must make. The reader is encouraged early to identify with Peter, then "stay with Peter" throughout the course of Peter's theological "conversion." The reader who successfully maintains this identification is shaped by the narrative to accept the theological convictions of the implied author.

Peter's preeminence among the disciples. Luke's plotting of the story establishes Peter's preeminence among the disciples from the first. Mark's story named four disciples—Simon, Andrew, James, and John—in the initial call scene and placed all four in "the house of Simon and Andrew" (Mk. 1:19–20, 29). Luke's story puts singular focus on Peter. After scenes in the synagogues in Nazareth and Capernaum, Jesus enters "Simon's house" and heals Simon's mother-in-law; Andrew, James, and John receive no mention. Later Jesus is standing by the lake of Gennesaret with the crowd gathering around to hear him teach. Jesus sees two boats and gets into "the one belonging to Simon" (Lk. 5:3).

Peter's call. Even more remarkable is the call of Peter in Luke. The Marcan Jesus had called Simon and Andrew with the words, "Follow me and I will make you fish for people" (Mk. 1:17). Luke expands this saying of Jesus' into an enacted parable. Jesus instructs Simon alone to put out into deep water and let down the nets for a catch. Simon obeys and, along with his unnamed partners, "they" brought in such a multitude of fish that the nets began to tear and they "signaled their partners in the other boat to come and help them" (Lk. 5:7).

Simon Peter's response to the catch is of particular significance: "But when Simon Peter saw it, he fell down at Jesus' knees, saying, 'Go away from me, Lord, for I am a sinful man'" (Lk. 5:8). These words characterize Peter in a way that reminds the reader of the Hebrew prophets. Isaiah had responded to his vision in the temple saying, "Woe is me! I am lost, for I am a man of unclean lips, and I live among a people of unclean lips; yet my eyes have seen the King, the LORD of hosts!" (Isa. 6:5). Peter responds similarly to his encounter with someone he recognizes from the first as "Lord."

Only after this remarkable call story does the reader learn the identity of Simon's partners, James and John; Andrew receives no mention. The scene concludes with the words of Jesus' call, directed here singularly to Peter, not to a group of four: "Then Jesus said to Simon, 'Do not be afraid; from now on you will be catching people'" (Lk. 5:10). Luke's readers hold the figure of Peter in high estimation, and Luke's characterization of Peter in the call story plays into their values and encourages them to hold this exalted view.

Peter's confession. Luke continues to treat the character of Peter with extraordinary care. The Marcan story treated Peter quite harshly in the aftermath of the confession. Peter responded to the first prediction of Jesus' passion by "rebuking" Jesus; in response Jesus "rebuked Peter and said, 'Get behind me, Satan!'" (Mk. 8:33). When the Lucan Jesus responds to Peter's confession with a prophecy of the passion, the narrative outcome is entirely different. Peter does not rebuke these words of Jesus. Neither does Jesus call Peter "Satan" (see Lk. 9:22 ff.).

Jesus predicts Peter's denial. In the plotting of Mark's story, the denial pericope becomes the ultimate failure of Peter's discipleship. Luke's treatment of the denial gives Peter the benefit of a highly positive spin. Notice that immediately before Jesus predicts Peter's denial, he affirms the faithfulness of his disciples and confers honor on them: "You are those who have stood by me in my trials; and I confer on you, just as my Father has conferred on me, a kingdom, so that you may eat and drink at my table in my kingdom, and you will sit on thrones judging the twelve tribes of Israel" (Lk. 22:28–30). Moreover, Jesus predicts the denial in a way that puts Peter in a favorable light.

> "Simon, Simon, listen! Satan has demanded to sift all of you like wheat, but I have prayed for you that your own faith may not fail; and you, when once you have turned back, strengthen your brothers." And he said to him, "Lord, I am ready to go with you to prison and to death!" Jesus said, "I tell you, Peter, the cock will not crow this day, until you have denied three times that you know me." (Lk. 22: 31–34)

First, Peter and all of the disciples will face a trial by Satan. Second, Jesus prays that Peter's faith will not fail him because of that trial. Third, Jesus predicts that Peter will turn back in the aftermath of the trial.[11] Fourth, Jesus gives Peter a mission, the specific task of strengthening his brothers after he has turned back.[12] It is only in this carefully constructed context that Peter's denial is predicted. The reader already knows that Peter will face the opposition of Satan, that Peter's faith will not fail. He *will* turn back with the mission of strengthening the other disciples.

In Gethsemane. In both the Marcan and Matthean versions of the Gethsemane pericope, Jesus found the disciples asleep *three* times; Peter is personally criticized for not keeping awake (Mt. 26:40–41; Mk. 14:37–38). In Luke, Jesus finds the disciples asleep only *once*, and Peter is *not* singled out by Jesus. The disciples are not criticized

---

[11]Luke uses the verb *epistrepho* with the sense of repentance (Lk. 17:4) and turning to God (Lk. 1:16; Acts 3:19; 9:35; 11:21; 14:15; 15:19; 26:18, 20; 28:27).

[12]Luke uses the same verb, *sterizo*, in Luke 9:51 where Jesus "strengthened" his face (steeled his resolve) to go to Jerusalem. Peter is called to steel the resolve of his fellow disciples.

for their inability to keep awake for one hour; Jesus simply asks, "Why are you sleeping?" The narrator has already provided an exculpatory explanation; they are "sleeping because of grief" (Lk. 22:45–46).

The denial. It is helpful to compare Luke's account with how Matthew and Mark told the story. When Jesus was arrested, the disciples deserted him and fled (Mt. 26:56; Mk. 14:50). Jesus was immediately brought before the council and put on trial. There he was condemned to death, physically insulted, and taunted. At the very moment in which Jesus was literally slapped in the face by the court, he was figuratively slapped in the face by Peter, who denied him three times. Peter's denial becomes the ultimate insult in this chain of indignities.

Luke's plotting of the story is quite different. When Jesus is arrested, the disciples do *not* desert him or flee. Jesus is taken to the high priest's house, but the trial does not begin immediately; this movement merely establishes the setting for the denial. Peter's denial takes place *before* the beginning of Jesus' trials before the council, Pilate, and Herod. We read the account of this painful moment in Peter's discipleship with the words of Jesus' prophecy still in our ears. We know that while Peter will be tested, his faith will not fail; he will turn back and strengthen his brothers. When the cock crowed, "the Lord turned and looked at Peter. Then Peter remembered the word of the Lord...And he went out and wept bitterly" (Lk. 22:61–62). The reader is left with a clear impression: This has been a painful test, but Peter and Jesus remain in relationship.[13]

---

[13] A feminist reading of the denial narratives yields interesting results. In Mark's story, the servant-girl confronts Peter, and he denies her truthful allegation. She nevertheless confronts him a second time, characterizing her as an extraordinarily strong woman. Matthew's story put the second challenge on the lips of "another servant-girl," avoiding such a strong characterization of an individual woman (Mt. 26:71). Luke attributes the second and third challenges to *men*, changing the gender-based dynamics of the story entirely. Peter presumably loses less honor in losing a challenge that comes primarily from men.

Notice as well that Luke has reversed the order of the Marcan denials. The Marcan narrative puts Peter's most damning words at the final, climactic position in the series of three denials. Luke puts the statement at the beginning of the series, softening its dramatic impact. Whereas the Marcan Peter is confronted with being an associate of "Jesus, the man from Nazareth" (Mk. 14:67), Peter's accusers in Luke never confront him with the name of Jesus. The Lucan Peter is accused of being "with him" and replies, with some degree of ambiguity, "Woman, I do not know him" (Lk. 22:56–57). Finally, the impact of Peter's statement in Mark—"Neither do I know [him], nor do I understand what you are talking about" (Mk. 14:68, author trans.)—is blunted considerably; Luke's Peter says, "I do not know what you are talking about" (Lk. 22:60).

Peter at the empty tomb. While neither Peter nor any of the disciples appear again in Mark's story, Peter plays a prominent role in the Lucan resurrection story. The women return from the empty tomb with the message "that the Son of Man must be handed over to sinners, and be crucified, and on the third day rise" (Lk. 24:7). The women tell the apostles, "but these words seemed to them an idle tale, and they did not believe them. *But Peter* got up and ran to the tomb; stooping and looking in, he saw the linen cloths by themselves; then he went home, amazed at what had happened" (Lk. 24:11–12, emphasis mine). While the others do not believe the women, Peter apparently does, becoming the first apostle to believe. The first Easter proclamation of the eleven emphasizes Peter's prominent role: "The Lord has risen indeed, *and he has appeared to Simon!*" (Lk. 24:34, emphasis mine).

Peter's role in the beginning of Acts. Peter was instrumental in strengthening his brothers following the resurrection. His role becomes preeminent in the beginning of Acts. Within the story level of the narrative, Peter becomes the prophetic interpreter of the events that took place on Pentecost. Three thousand individuals believed and were baptized into the church as the result of his preaching. At the discourse level of the narrative, Peter is the spokesperson for the implied author; his sermon directly conveys Luke's theological argument.

Peter is characterized as a decisive leader of the church. His proposal to choose a twelfth apostle is accepted (Acts 1:15–26), and he deals with the incident involving Ananias and Sapphira (Acts 5:1–11). Peter continues to be the major actor on the narrative stage, healing a man who was lame from birth, preaching to the people from the portico of the temple, boldly defying the council, even being delivered from prison by an angel. In fact, Peter comes to be venerated by the people of Jerusalem: "They even carried out the sick into the streets, and laid them on cots and mats, in order that Peter's shadow might fall on some of them as he came by" (Acts 5:15).[14]

Peter's role in the transition to the Gentile ministry. I have discussed earlier Peter's role in the Cornelius narrative. All of the preceding

---

[14]This is even more extraordinary than the veneration shown Jesus (Lk. 6:19; 18:15). People sought to "touch" Jesus to receive healing; they sought healing from Peter's "shadow."

character development has prepared the reader for this transition. Peter has been first among the disciples since his call. He is the one who confessed Jesus as Messiah, the one whom Jesus prophesied would strengthen his brothers, the first to respond positively to the resurrection message. He has been a preeminent figure in the Jerusalem church, its greatest preacher, and its leader in the face of its first crises. Peter now becomes the one who receives the vision that opens the door for Jewish Christians to take the gospel to the Gentiles. Moreover, Peter initiates the Gentile ministry and orders the baptism of Cornelius and his household, the first Gentile believers. Finally, Peter is allied with Paul in the dispute that is brought to the Jerusalem Conference.

Homiletical reflections. Luke–Acts successfully affects the reader who identifies with Peter and maintains that identification throughout the course of Peter's transformation. Preachers can exploit this capacity of narrative. Our appeal is not only to the mind through the force of our ideas. We can appeal to the heart, to the imagination, through the compelling characterization of the folks who populate the biblical story. "When we identify with a character in a story," Thomas Long reminds us, "whatever happens to that character happens to us at the level of imagination."[15]

Dramatic moments in Peter's career give the preacher the opportunity to explore the nature of Christian discipleship. At his call, Peter, confronted with God's power, responded with awe. Like Moses, Isaiah, Jeremiah, and many other figures in Israel's story, Peter resisted that call because of a sense that he was unworthy and inadequate for the task. In the story that follows, we see Peter's often painful process of growth, through which he develops adequacy, eventually becoming the early church's prophet, visionary, and leader. The denial story plays a critical role in Peter's development as a "wounded healer."[16] Luke offers a sympathetic view of the role of suffering and failure in our formation as disciples. Peter learned to face his own failure. Peter learned that, even in the moment of his

---

[15]Thomas G. Long, *Preaching and the Literary Forms of the Bible* (Philadelphia: Fortress Press, 1989), 75.

[16]This is the memorable expression of Henri J. M. Nouwen in *The Wounded Healer: Ministry in Contemporary Society* (Garden City, N.Y.: Doubleday, 1972).

deepest failure, Jesus looked *at* him, not *away from* him. Peter's failure enabled him to look at others and their failures with compassion. It empowered him to become the decisive leader the church needed.

Summary. Peter is paradigmatic of a Jewish Christian who successfully resolves his anti-Gentile aversion. Peter comes to understand that God's purpose is to use Israel to bless "all the families of the earth" (Acts 3:25). Peter will initiate the Gentile mission in his visit to Cornelius, but the problem of table fellowship with Gentiles remains a serious obstacle to such a mission. Peter demonstrates the natural aversion of the implied reader to the idea of eating unkosher food, or having table fellowship with those who do, but that aversion is overcome in the vision he receives (Acts 10:9–16). His new understanding is made explicit in Acts 10:34–36. "I truly understand that God shows no partiality, but in every nation anyone who fears him and does what is right is acceptable to him. You know the message he sent to the people of Israel, preaching peace by Jesus Christ—he is Lord of all." Thus, Peter is "converted" to the viewpoint of the implied author.

Who is the Implied Reader of Luke–Acts?

While Luke has traditionally been considered the gospel to the Gentiles, the setting and characterization of the main figures in Luke-Acts are what would be expected given a Jewish audience. The gospel of Luke, for instance, begins its plot by focusing on a priest performing his priestly duties; the setting is the temple in Jerusalem, in the holy of holies. The gospel ends with the disciples in the same setting, having returned to Jerusalem where "they were continually in the temple blessing God" (Lk. 24:53). I have already noted that Luke consistently portrays major figures in the narrative as pious, observant Jews. The Acts of the Apostles likewise opens in Jerusalem; this setting is made explicit by the fact that Jesus "ordered them not to leave Jerusalem" (Acts 1:4). The daily life of the disciples is centered in the temple (Acts 2:46).

I contend that the implied readers of Luke–Acts are Jewish Christians resisting association with Gentile believers within the church. Such a reader would view the historical figure of Peter favorably and invest Peter with considerable authority. Luke exploits the reader's natural tendency to identify with Peter, gaining the reader's allegiance by his positive characterization of Peter. Luke's rhetorical strategy is that the reader remain identified with Peter throughout his theological transformation. If the narrative is successful, Luke will have persuaded the implied reader of his own theological perspective.

Preaching Luke–Acts

There are both advantages and disadvantages to lectionary preaching. The lectionary offers preachers the opportunity to work intentionally with a given gospel over the course of an entire year. It disciplines us to consider a wider scope of texts than we normally might preach from. It makes it more likely that we will begin our sermon preparation by focusing on a biblical text and seeking to hear its message, rather than by beginning with a message and searching for a text.

At the same time, preachers need to be aware that the lectionary itself represents a particular reading of a gospel. The committee's choice of which texts to include or leave out is itself an interpretation of the gospel. This makes it all the more critical that preachers spend time with the story-as-a-whole. Preaching the lectionary is not an adequate substitute for reading and interpreting the gospel.

The Revised Common Lectionary (1992) does not assign Peter's confession in the gospel of Luke (Lk. 9:18–20) to any of the Sundays in year C. Nevertheless, when we preach from Luke–Acts, our telling of the story of Jesus should incorporate the confession *as Luke tells it*. Perhaps we will depart from the lectionary on occasion to preach from crucial Lucan texts that the lectionary leaves out.

Brainstorming and Researching Luke–Acts

I am beginning my homiletical analysis by reading the confession in light of the story-as-a-whole. That story begins before Jesus' conception and ends with Paul preaching in Rome. The plot of Luke–Acts is organized in terms of its geographical agenda:

Galilean Ministry	Journey to Jerusalem	Jerusalem	Judea and Samaria	Gentile Ministry
Lk. 4:14—9:50	*Lk. 9:51—19:27*	*Lk. 19:28—Acts 8:1a*	*Acts 8:1b—9:43*	*Acts 10—28*

Each broad change of narrative setting as shown above leads to a turn in the plot. The public ministry of Jesus begins in the synagogue at Nazareth, eventually encompassing the "cities and villages" of Galilee (Lk. 8:1). As 9:1–27 begins, the Galilean ministry now involves the Twelve who are preaching and healing in villages everywhere (Lk. 9:6). The ministry has extended to the widest potential geographical range in its Galilean setting.

The confession effects a major turn in the plot's direction. When Jesus is acknowledged by Peter to be "the Messiah of God" (Lk. 9:20), now of necessity Jesus must "undergo great suffering, and be rejected by the elders, chief priests, and scribes, and be killed, and on the third day be raised" (Lk. 9:22). As these events will take place not in Galilee, but Jerusalem (where the antagonists are), the plot must now move Jesus to this ultimate setting. The confession is the "hinge" on which the plot turns. Jesus leaves Galilee and begins his extended journey to Jerusalem, a major movement in the plot of Luke–Acts.

In addition to this wide-angle view of Luke–Acts, I want to read the confession in its immediate literary context. A pericope's co-text is usually an important clue to its interpretation. Because Luke has deleted a major block of Marcan material (Mk. 6:45—8:27a) from the narrative, the confession takes place in an entirely different context in Luke's gospel. Peter's confession is preceded by the feeding of the five thousand (Lk. 9:11–17) and Herod's perplexity (Lk. 9:7–9). The three pericopae are linked chiastically:

> A $\Big\{$
>   a Herod's perplexity (9:7a)
>   b John, Elijah, a prophet arose (9:7b–8)
>   c Herod's question: Who then is this? (9:9)
>   B Jesus withdraws with the apostles (9:10)
>   X Feeding the five thousand (9:11–17)
>   B' Jesus prays alone with the disciples (9:18a)
> A' $\Big\{$
>   c' Jesus' question: Who do the crowds say I am? (9:18b)
>   b' John, Elijah, a prophet arose (9:19)
>   a' Peter's confession (9:20)

Herod's perplexity. Notice that the stories of Herod's perplexity (A) and Peter's confession (A') are structured in an inversely parallel fashion. Herod's perplexity begins by noting (a) Herod's perplexity in the context of (b) the reports he has heard concerning the identity of Jesus. This leads to (c) the articulation of Herod's question, "Who then is this?" Peter's confession begins with (c') Jesus' question to his disciples, "Who do the crowds say that I am?" This is followed by (b') the disciples' report of what they have heard from the crowds (a report identical to that given Herod). It concludes with (a') Peter's confession that Jesus is the Messiah. Luke highlights the stark contrast between Peter's insight and Herod's perplexity.

The feeding of the five thousand. The feeding pericope is at the center of the chiasm and thus represents its "conceptual center," the hermeneutical key for the entire rhetorical unit.[17] The crowds have followed Jesus into a desert place. Jesus welcomed them and "spoke to them about the kingdom of God" (Lk. 9:11). The dramatic action of feeding the crowd portrays a common first-century understanding of the kingdom as the restoration of the twelve tribes.[18] Jesus' action of raising up twelve baskets of fragments is a sign of the restoration of the twelve tribes of Israel. This action is instrumental in *this* narrative in bringing Peter to the understanding of Jesus' identity expressed in the christological title *Messiah of God.*[19]

Other Narrative Links

There are any number of narrative links that can profitably be explored. I find two links in particular to be especially helpful. I will discuss the relationship of Peter's confession with the Emmaus Road pericope (Lk. 24:13–32) and with the story of Peter and Cornelius (Acts 10).

The Emmaus Road encounter. Luke has placed the confession immediately after the feeding of the five thousand. The feeding describes Jesus' actions of taking, blessing, and breaking bread (Lk. 9:16). This set of actions occurs at three other places in Luke–Acts, one of them being the Emmaus Road episode.[20] Though the Emmaus disciples have been walking and talking with the risen Jesus, they do not

---

[17]John Breck, "Biblical Chiasmus: Exploring Structure for Meaning," *Biblical Theology Bulletin* 17 (1987): 73.

[18]E. P. Sanders, *Jesus and Judaism* (Philadelphia: Fortress Press, 1985), 97.

[19]See Robert C. Tannehill's discussion of the relationship of the feeding and the confession in *The Narrative Unity of Luke–Acts: A Literary Interpretation.* Vol. 1. *The Gospel According to Luke* (Philadelphia: Fortress Press, 1986), 214–15.

[20]These actions are found at Luke 9:16; 22:19; 24:30; and Acts 27:35.

recognize him. Reaching their village, they invite him into their home. "When he was at the table with them, he took bread, blessed and broke it, and gave it to them. Then their eyes were opened, and they recognized him" (Lk. 24:30–31). Luke makes the point explicit: Jesus is recognized in the breaking of the bread. Peter's eyes were opened as well when Jesus broke bread at the feeding of the five thousand.[21]

Peter and Cornelius. Peter affirms at Luke 9:20 that Jesus is "the Messiah of God." This confession comes at a key turning point in the plot of Luke as Jesus leaves Galilee and begins his journey to Jerusalem. In his confession at Luke 9:20, Peter conveys a valid but partial understanding of Jesus' identity: Jesus is the Messiah long expected by the Jews. Peter's consummate expression of Jesus' identity comes at Acts 10:36. Speaking to Cornelius, Peter declares, "Jesus the Messiah—he is Lord of all" (author trans.). Jesus is more than the long-awaited Jewish Messiah; he is indeed Lord of *all*. The Cornelius pericope provides the narrative justification for table fellowship between Jews and Gentiles, a practical precondition for the Gentile ministry. In combination with this event, Peter's accompanying confession that this one "is Lord of all" satisfies a christological precondition to permit the ministry to the Gentiles to begin.

There are a number of interesting parallels between the confessions in Luke 9 and Acts 10. First, while the setting of the Lucan confession is left ambiguous (Luke does *not* locate Peter's confession at Caesarea Philippi), the confession in Acts 10 is set explicitly in a place explicitly identified as Caesarea. While the Caesarea of Acts is not Caesarea Philippi but Caesarea Maritima, it is intriguing that Peter's consummate confession would take place in a setting Luke–Acts identifies as Caesarea.

Second, Herod was perplexed (*diaporeo*) on hearing reports of the results of the ministry of the Twelve (Lk. 9:7). In Acts 10:17, Peter is perplexed (*diaporeo*) by the vision of unkosher food and by God's apparent message to him: "Kill and eat...What *God* has made clean, *you* do not declare unclean" (Acts 10:13, 15, author trans.).

---

[21]John Drury, *Tradition and Design in Luke's Gospel: A Study in Early Christian Historiography* (Atlanta: John Knox Press, 1976), 101.

Just as the reports of Jesus' ministry shattered Herod's construct of reality, Peter's vision represents for him (and the implied reader) a world-shattering metaphor.

Third, both confessions take place in the context of meals. The feeding of the five thousand is initiated by the disciples' desire to "send the crowd away" that they may find lodging and provisions (Lk. 9:12). Though Peter in Acts 10 is hungry, he is inclined to reject the meal offered in his vision. Despite their initial disinclination in both stories, Peter and the disciples receive commands (the imperative is used) in both Luke 9 and Acts 10. As a result of these commands, meals take place that are described in Luke and implied in Acts.[22] What is significant is that in both meal-related contexts—the feeding and the vision—Peter realizes a fuller understanding of the identity and mission of Jesus. After the feeding, Peter confesses Jesus as "Messiah of God." After the vision, Peter confesses Jesus as "Lord of all."

Establishing the Sermon's Plotline

The confession pericope in Luke is set within a narrative distinctly different from the gospel of Mark. Most pointedly, Luke–Acts does *not* function to discredit Peter and the disciples. Luke's gospel characterizes Peter in a positive fashion, for Luke–Acts will exploit the referent power the implied reader attributed to Peter. His authority will be used to add credibility to the theological argument made overtly in the sermons attributed to him in Acts as well as by the narrative itself. Consequently, a sermon on Peter's confession, developed in light of a narrative analysis of Luke–Acts, will not question Peter's discipleship.

---

[22]The implied author introduces a gap into the narrative in Acts. Peter receives Cornelius' emissaries as his guests; does he feed and/or eat with them? Cornelius invites Peter to be his guest for several days; does Peter accept and eat with him? Can we imagine that Peter would have dishonored the one he had just baptized by refusing a reciprocal invitation? Although Peter is "hungry and wanted something to eat" (Acts 10:10) and is in the company of Cornelius and/or his associates for *at least* the next three days, the narrative never shows him eating during this entire period. Peter is then asked in Acts 11:2 why he ate with the uncircumcised, but his reply never acknowledges or denies that he did. Thus, the implied author is allowed to remain "on the fence" while the implied reader must draw a conclusion based on the evidence in the story.

The following sermon employs a chiastic (or concentric) structure:

A Whom to sit next to at the counter in the diner
    B Peter offers hospitality to Gentiles and accepts the hospitality of Cornelius (Acts 10:1–33)
        C The Emmaus disciples offer hospitality to a stranger (Lk 24:13–29)
            D The disciples offer their food to the crowds (Lk 9:10–17)
                X Eucharist and being open to the mystery of God
            D' Peter recognizes Jesus as "Messiah of God" (Lk 9:18–20)
        C' The Emmaus disciples recognize the stranger (Lk. 24:30–32)
    B' Peter recognizes Jesus as "Lord of all" (Acts 10:34–36)
A' Whom to sit next to at the counter in the diner

Although the sermon is structurally symmetrical, the large majority of the sermon's time is devoted to the first half of the chiasm, which establishes and develops sermonic tension. The clue to resolution is found at the crux of the chiasm—eucharist and being open to the mystery of God. This occurs nearly four-fifths of the way into the sermon.

Disequilibrium. I use a contemporary image to "upset the equilibrium." I understand Luke–Acts as being addressed to traditional Jewish Christians who are averse to the growing presence of Gentile Christians in the church. In Luke–Acts, this aversion takes on particularity around the issue of table fellowship between Jews and Gentiles. As this is not a live issue among contemporary Christians, I have described a parallel situation with which contemporary listeners can identify.

I develop the tension ("analyze the discrepancy") with three episodes from Luke–Acts: Peter and Cornelius, the Emmaus Road encounter, and Peter's confession (which, in Luke, immediately follows the feeding of the five thousand). In each episode, table fellowship takes place under extraordinary circumstances. Peter accepts the hospitality of Cornelius, a Gentile; the Emmaus disciples offer hospitality to a stranger they meet on the road; and the disciples feed the crowd despite their stated wish to send them away to find provisions for themselves. The reader will note that the sermon moves through these episodes in reverse chronological order. In other words, I plot the sermon differently than Luke plots his narrative.

Resolution. I find the sermon's "clue to resolution" in a literary feature of the narrative: in Luke–Acts, Peter's confession immediately follows the feeding of the five thousand. This pericope, like the Emmaus Road encounter, uses explicitly eucharistic language. Just as with the Emmaus disciples, Peter is able to understand Jesus in the context of a eucharistic event.

The sermon's first half plotted the three episodes in reverse order in order to delay for as long as possible my introduction of the Feeding pericope and its key to the sermon's resolution. Now that the sermon's "Aha!" moment has been reached, the sermon's second half moves quickly through all three episodes, now following Luke's chronological order. In each case, I describe how extraordinary table fellowship has enabled disciples to "experience the gospel." Eyes, minds, and hearts have been opened by an act of grace. The sermon concludes with a reprise of the opening contemporary image, but things have now changed for the listeners, who are able to "anticipate the consequences" of affirming that Jesus is Lord of all.

Being Open to Contemporary Images

Table fellowship is an important theme throughout Luke–Acts. Luke wants Jewish Christians to accept table fellowship with Gentile Christians. However, the issue stated this way does not speak to the situation of a contemporary audience. Therefore, it is necessary to propose a contemporary image to which a congregation can relate. I introduce the image of a lunch counter at a diner. My listeners are asked to imagine themselves in the situation of needing to decide whom to sit next to at the diner. The image helps members of the congregation to be in touch with the natural reticence they may feel at the thought of sitting next to strangers.

I weave another contemporary image into my discussion of the feeding of the five thousand. It is late in the day, and the disciples want to send the crowd away to get provisions for themselves. While I want the congregation to relate to the disciples, listeners may be reluctant to relate to characters whose behavior is challenged by Jesus. Thus, I introduce the image of church members who become

highly conscious of time when a worship service goes past the ap-
pointed "hour." Humor can be a useful strategy for the preacher. If
the congregation can laugh at their own similarity to the disciples,
they have successfully identified with the disciples in the story.

Weaving the Sermon

The sermon weaves together threads of the three biblical stories
and two contemporary images I have just described. Each biblical
story in the thread relates table fellowship (the breaking of bread)
with a recognition or deepening understanding of who Jesus is. I
use a simple narrative pattern—a chiasm—to unify the narrative
elements of the sermon.

❖

A Not Insignificant Decision
Luke 9:10–20

A

You walk into a diner to grab a quick lunch.
All the tables are occupied,
    but there are a number of open spaces at the counter.
You glance quickly at the people sitting there
    so that you can decide where to sit…
        or, more precisely, whom to sit next to.
Your eyes take in all sorts of information…
    age, gender, race, ethnicity,
    how well the diner is dressed,
    how well groomed she may be,
    is his body pierced? how many times?
    and in what places?
The choice of a dining companion
  is a not insignificant decision.
        It makes us quite conscious of our prejudices…
            with whom would you be comfortable
            breaking bread?

B

That question is close to the heart of Luke's concern.
Breaking bread is one of the most intimate forms of human
  interaction,
        and the question of what to eat,
        and with whom to eat it,
            runs through Luke-Acts.
In the tenth chapter of Acts,
        a God-fearing Gentile named Cornelius
        receives a vision.
An angel of God addresses him by name,
        tells him that his prayers and alms
        have been received by God,
            and instructs him to seek out one Simon Peter
                who, at that time, is in Joppa.
Cornelius sends two messengers.
The scene shifts.
It is noon the following day. We are in Joppa.
We see Peter go up to the roof of the house to pray.
He is hungry and wants something to eat.
While lunch is being prepared, Peter falls into a trance.
        He sees a strange vision.
            A large sheet is lowered from heaven.
                On the sheet are all kinds
                of four-footed creatures and reptiles
                and birds of the air.
Peter hears a strange command:
        "Get up, Peter; kill and eat."
Peter refuses:
        "By no means, Lord,
        for I have never eaten anything profane or unclean."
The voice insists:
        "What God has made clean, you must not call profane."
Three times this exchange takes place,
        and the sheet is suddenly taken up to heaven.
Peter is greatly perplexed.

The scene shifts again.
We're back downstairs.
The two messengers from Cornelius have arrived.
They tell Peter of the vision Cornelius has received
    instructing him to send for Peter.
Peter invites the two messengers into the house and offers
   them hospitality…
      which seems unremarkable
      until you recall the cast of characters:
         Peter—the observant Jew
         who has never violated the kosher laws
         and two slaves of Cornelius,
            not only a Gentile
            but an officer in the hated Roman Army.
Peter offers them hospitality.
The choice of a dinner companion—or house guest—
    is a not insignificant decision.
It makes us quite conscious of our own prejudices…
    with whom would you be comfortable breaking bread?
And, of course, the story goes on.
Next day, Peter goes with the two slaves
   to the town of Caesarea.
Peter is welcomed rather lavishly by Cornelius
     and invited into his home,
       where many are assembled.
Peter addresses the audience
     and just in case the reader doesn't "get it,"
     just in case we don't notice
     how momentous an act this is,
     Luke spells it out for us in black and white:
"You yourselves know," Peter says to his audience,
"that it is unlawful for a Jew
    to associate with or to visit a Gentile,
but God has shown me
    I should not call anyone profane or unclean."
The choice of a dinner companion,
   or house guest, or congregation
    is a not insignificant decision.
It makes us keenly aware of our own prejudices…

C

All kinds of significant decisions take place in Luke–Acts
    when bread is broken in unusual circumstances.
Remember the story?
Two of Jesus' followers
    are traveling to a village seven miles from Jerusalem.
As they journey on, they are joined by a stranger.
A perfect stranger…
        what kinds of fears rise up in our hearts
            when we're approached by someone we don't know
                in an isolated place far from safety?
But the disciples engage the stranger in conversation
    and discuss with him
        the strange goings-on of the past few days:
 Though their grief is still intense,
        they pour out their hearts to the stranger,
            telling how Jesus was crucified,
            dashing their hopes,
            how the women saw a vision that Jesus was alive.
        But when the disciples went to the tomb,
        they did not see him.
A perfect stranger.
    They offer him hospitality.
    They invite him to stay in their home.
    They break bread together,
And the stranger "took bread, blessed and broke it, and gave
    it to them."
The choice of a dinner companion, or house guest,
        the choice of a partner in a conversation about God
        and about the deepest secrets of our hearts
            is a not insignificant decision.
It brings us painfully in touch with our own prejudices…

D

"*You* give them something to eat."
That isn't quite what the disciples have in mind.
The crowds have followed them into the wilderness,
        and Jesus has welcomed them,
        and taught them about the kingdom of God,

and healed those who needed to be cured.
But the disciples have their eyes on the clock,
    or, rather, the sun,
        which is soon going to set.
Practical-minded as they are,
    they suggest it's time to dismiss the crowd,
        so they can get themselves something to eat,
        so they can get on the road before dark.
That's what the disciples have in mind...
    The crowds have heard the sermon
    and had a healing service;
        now it's time to say the benediction
            and send them back out into the world.
The disciples are more than a little annoyed
    by all these simple people
    who tag along wherever they go,
        not giving them a moment to themselves.
The crowds sure get to be a bother after a while,
    and the disciples want their private time with Jesus.
You know how antsy we church people can get
    when things go overtime,
        and the service has lasted well over an hour now.
But Jesus has something else in mind.
It's Communion Sunday.
"You give them something to eat."
All they have is the bread and the fish
    they've brought for themselves,
        their own dinner.
"And taking the five loaves and the two fish,
    he looked up to heaven,
    and blessed and broke them,
        and gave them to the disciples to set before the crowd."
The choice of dinner companions
    is a not insignificant decision.
To share your table, your own food,
    with five thousand men,
        not counting women and children,
            is an extraordinary thing.

X

Luke reminds us that our eyes and minds and hearts
    are opened to the mystery of God in many ways…
        • not just by hearing Jesus
           teach about the kingdom of God
           and explain the scriptures
        • not just by experiencing God's healing in our lives
        • not just by seeing visions
but by the experience of breaking bread.

D'

Jesus took bread and blessed and broke it
    and more than five thousand were fed,
        with more food left over than they had to begin with.
The disciples' eyes were opened.
"Who do you say that I am?"
    Jesus asks in the very next paragraph.
"The Messiah of God," answers Peter,
    the one Israel has been expecting.

C'

The stranger took bread
  and blessed and broke it and gave it to them,
    and the eyes of the Emmaus disciples were opened,
      and they recognized the risen Christ.

B'

Peter accepted the hospitality of a Gentile household,
    breaking bread with people
    no longer considered unclean,
      and his mind and heart were opened.
And he saw who Jesus was in the fullest sense.
"Jesus Christ," he said to Cornelius, "he is Lord of all."
    Not just Israel's Messiah but the Lord of all humankind.
Lord of *all*…
    of Jews and Gentiles,
    of strangers on the road,
    of hungry crowds,
    of pierced and unpierced alike.

Just as the angel promised
   "good news of great joy for all the people,"
  Peter confesses that Jesus, the Messiah of Israel,
  is Lord of all.
Of all.

A'

So you stand there in the diner,
   considering your possible dinner companions.
Your eyes take in all sorts of information…
    age and gender, race and ethnicity,
    how they are dressed,
    how they are groomed.
The choice of a dining companion
  is a not insignificant decision.
Whenever we break bread, it is a not insignificant event…
    whether we're seated next to a stranger
    at a lunch counter,
    whether we're gathered around the Lord's table,
     it is a not insignificant event.
It is a time to remember Jesus' death until he comes again
  and we can all sit at table *together* in the kingdom.
It is a time to remember that Jesus, the Messiah of God,
  is Lord of *all*.

Reflection on the Sermon

*You walk into a diner to grab a quick lunch…*The sermon begins and ends with a contemporary image. Members of the congregation are invited to imagine themselves going into a diner to eat and finding empty spaces at the counter. They face a common decision—whom to sit next to. This is a commonplace occurrence as we go through our days and have incidental contact with those we encounter. I allow the emotional content of such decisions, which is analogous to one of the major themes in Luke–Acts, to upset the equilibrium. I close this section of the sermon with a hint of where I am going by introducing a phrase with strong eucharistic overtones: "breaking bread."

*That question is close to the heart of Luke's concern…*Luke's narrative addresses a growing problem in the church—a problem arising from the natural aversion of Jewish Christians to Gentile Christians. This problem comes to a crisis in Acts 10. I retell the story, emphasizing how the Jewish–Gentile dynamics affect Peter. (I tell the story in the present tense throughout the first half of the sermon to encourage my congregation to experience the crisis of these events in a more immediate way.) I focus on the perplexing message Peter receives in his vision, on Peter's offering hospitality to Gentile emissaries sent by Cornelius, and on Peter's accepting the hospitality of Cornelius, a Gentile. I conclude with Peter's own words, which emphasize in stark terms the issue that is at stake. I leave the story at this point, with the tension unresolved.

*All kinds of significant decisions take place in Luke–Acts…*I move next to the story of the Emmaus Road encounter between two disciples and the risen Christ. Taking my clue from Cleopas' own words, I characterize the episode as an encounter with a stranger (Lk. 24:18). In my telling of the story, I allow my congregation to imagine the natural fear we would experience were we to be approached by a stranger in an isolated place. Beyond this, I remind my listeners of our natural reluctance to share intimacies with strangers. Moreover, the Emmaus disciples offer hospitality to the stranger. While their behavior may have been normal in their own cultural setting, it would be quite extraordinary in ours. I allow this anomaly to add to the sermonic tension.

"You give them something to eat…" I move, finally, to the feeding of the five thousand. Because I want the congregation to identify with the transformation experienced by the disciples, I tell the story in such a way that the congregation can identify with the disciples' desire to send away the crowds. I use humor, allowing listeners to relate the disciples' annoyance at the crowds to the congregation's own annoyance when worship begins to run overtime…and especially with the annoyance of some Protestant worshipers when communion lengthens the time spent in worship. I am "setting them up" so that they can hear, in Luke's narrative, how transformation takes place in breaking bread.

*Luke reminds us that our eyes and minds and hearts…*This is the sermon's clue to resolution, about four-fifths of the way into the sermon. I have intentionally kept the congregation's anticipation going for as long as possible. I make the point that grace comes about not just through preaching and healing but through breaking bread. To emphasize the point, I use a threefold repetition of phrases beginning with the words "not just." The eucharistic thread running through Luke–Acts, hinted at in the sermon's opening, is now made explicit.

Jesus took bread and blessed and broke it…Now that resolution has been provided, I move rapidly through the three Lucan pericopae and offer resolutions to the stories I have left hanging. The eucharistic experience of the feeding leads to Peter's confession of Jesus as "Messiah of God." The eucharistic experience on the Emmaus Road enables the two disciples to recognize the risen Christ. The experience of offering hospitality to, and receiving hospitality from, a Gentile enables Peter to recognize that Jesus is not just the Messiah long expected by Israel; Jesus is also the means by which God's blessing will reach all the world. Jesus is not just "Messiah" but "Lord of all." I briefly weave in another thread that relates this ultimate confession of Peter to the angel's promise in the Christmas story (Lk. 2:10).

So you stand there in the diner…The sermon's opening left the congregation standing in the diner considering the choice of possible dining companions. My listeners now return to that scene. I hope that their understanding of that choice has been transformed through the proclamation of the biblical story. While not intending to suggest that we need not be concerned about possible dangers, I invite the congregation to consider the many strangers we encounter—persons of all ages, genders, races, and ethnicity—to be children of God. I make an analogy between strangers seated at a lunch counter and worshipers gathered around the Lord's table. *Any* time we break bread together, whether in a secular or liturgical context, it is a time to remember Jesus, to anticipate the kingdom, and to celebrate God's love for *all* people.

4

Reading and Preaching the Gospel of Matthew

The decision of the canonizers to place the gospel of Matthew first in the New Testament has given this gospel profound influence in the church. Matthew's story presents Jesus as a new Moses, offers a summary of his teaching in five substantial discourses, and establishes the authority of the disciples to lead and teach the church. Although this gospel has a didactic purpose, it is set in narrative form. In this chapter, I will describe the narrative world that Matthew depicts.

As with the previous chapters, I will first develop a broad reading of the gospel's story-as-a-whole. I will then focus on Peter's confession as it is told by the gospel of Matthew. The material in this chapter has a dual purpose. First, it will document how I have moved from text to sermon in developing a message on the Matthean confession. Beyond this, I am hopeful that, intrigued by Matthew's story, the reader will engage the narrative itself.

Reading Matthew's Story

Matthew's narrative characterizes Jesus as the new Moses. As God revealed the Torah to Israel through Moses, so now Jesus is presented as the authoritative teacher and interpreter of the Torah. This concern is seen in the literary structure of the gospel. Five extended teaching discourses are embedded in the narrative: the sermon on the mount (Mt. 5—7), the missionary discourse (Mt. 8:1—10:4), the discourse in parables (Mt. 13:1–53), the community discourse (Mt. 18), and the closing eschatological discourse (Mt. 23—25). Bacon first proposed a five-part structure corresponding to the Five Books of Moses (also known as the Torah and the Pentateuch).[1]

I employ the following outline of Matthew for the discussion that follows:

Introduction: Matthew 1—2 (The Birth Narrative)

Book One
> Narrative: Matthew 3—4
> Discourse: Matthew 5—7 (The Sermon on the Mount)
>> ...*when Jesus had finished saying these things* (7:28)

Book Two
> Narrative: Matthew 8:1—10:4
> Discourse: Matthew 10:5–42 (The Missionary Discourse)
>> ...*when Jesus had finished instructing his twelve disciples* (11:1)

Book Three
> Narrative: Matthew 11—12
> Discourse: Matthew 13:1–53 (The Discourse in Parables)
>> ...*when Jesus had finished these parables* (13:53)

Book Four
> Narrative: Matthew 13:54—17:27
> Discourse: Matthew 18 (The Community Discourse)
>> ...*when Jesus had finished saying these things* (19:1)

Book Five
> Narrative: Matthew 19—22
> Discourse: Matthew 23—25 (The Eschatological Discourse)
>> ...*when Jesus had finished saying all these things* (26:1)

Conclusion: Matthew 26—28 (The Passion and Resurrection)

---

[1]Benjamin Bacon, *Studies in Matthew* (London: Constable, 1930). In further support of the idea that Matthew patterned his narrative with the Torah in mind, note that the gospel of Matthew and the Torah begin with the same words: *Biblos geneseos* (Gen. 1:1, LXX; Mt. 1:1).

There are two distinct features of this structure. First, Matthew consists of five "books," each containing a narrative section followed by an extended discourse. Second, each discourse ends with a similar phrase: *when Jesus had finished*...This phrase concludes the discourse and provides a transition into the subsequent section of narrative.

Why is Matthew telling the story of Jesus in this particular way? Like each of the evangelists, Matthew is addressing the missional needs of the church as he understands them. How does Matthew understand those needs?

(1) The church is facing a tremendous opportunity and requires more workers to carry out that mission. Within the story, Jesus feels compassion for the crowds who gather to hear him and seek healing. He sees them as "harassed and helpless, like sheep without a shepherd," and prays for more workers in the harvest (Mt. 9:36–38). Matthew concludes his narrative with his contemporary situation in mind: Jesus issues a clarion call, sending his disciples to "make disciples of all nations" (Mt. 28:19).

(2) Though the opportunity is great, potential workers are put off by the hardship of the mission. The mission suffers from a scarcity of workers. It is difficult to enlist workers for the missionary effort because of the hardships entailed by that work. The needs of an itinerant mission involve numerous sacrifices: leaving the comforts of home and family, enduring material scarcity, and facing the threat of persecution.

(3) Matthew understands the difficulty of enlisting workers for the mission to be the result of an inadequate understanding of Christian discipleship. Matthew argues against those within the church who have advocated a way that is easy and a gate that is broad. An adequate view of discipleship is one that acknowledges that "the gate is narrow and the road is hard that leads to life, and there are few who find it" (Mt. 7:14).

(4) While many within the church have been misled by false teachers who have promised an easy way, Matthew rejects the attitude of those who would simply "write off" these lost disciples. A church whose heart is filled with harsh judgmentalism cannot credibly bear the good news of God's

grace. Matthew calls the church to suspend judgment and
go to these lost sheep with mercy and a readiness to forgive.
(5) Matthew strongly criticizes his theological opponents beyond the church. His narrative personifies them as the scribes
and the pharisees.

The Plentiful Harvest

Matthew's gospel concludes with a clarion call for the church
to be about its mission (the great commission). The narrative's rhetorical strategy prepares the reader to take this calling to heart by
making the reader aware that the missional need is great. Within the
story, Jesus feels compassion for the crowds and sends the Twelve to
"the lost sheep of the house of Israel" (Mt. 10:5b). The need is equally
urgent in Matthew's own day.

The "crowds" in Matthew. Matthew plots his story and draws its
characters in a way that differs substantially from Mark. This is evi-
dent from the beginning of the account of Jesus' ministry. In Mark's
gospel, the response to Jesus' ministry is immediate, vocal, dramatic,
and enthusiastic. Demons in Mark know who Jesus is and identify
him openly. Crowds in Mark hear Jesus' teaching, witness his healing, and respond verbally from the beginning. Individuals in Mark
are healed and publicly proclaim what Jesus has done, even though
they are commanded to remain silent. The crowds in Mark quickly
become so numerous that Jesus cannot appear publicly (Mk. 1:45).

Jesus' ministry begins more quietly in Matthew's telling of the
story. Notice, first, that Matthew's story contains *no* references to
demons who know Jesus or who openly identify him. Second, the
response of the crowds is muted in Matthew. While the narrator
describes their reaction to Jesus, the crowds do not speak throughout the first eight chapters of Matthew's narrative. When verbal
responses from the crowd are finally reported in the ninth chapter,
the first three comments are critical remarks spoken by scribes (Mt.
9:3), pharisees (Mt. 9:11), and disciples of John (Mt. 9:14). The crowd's
first verbal acclamation of Jesus is not made until the conclusion of
the second narrative section (Mt. 9:33), and even this positive word
is paired with the negative response of the pharisees (Mt. 9:34).

Third, there is no indication in Matthew's narrative that large
crowds complicated Jesus' ministry or made his comings and goings

problematic. Consider the following details from the Marcan narrative, and consider that *each of the following narrative elements is absent from Matthew's story:*

- Mark reports, following the beginning of Jesus' public ministry in the synagogue at Capernaum, that "at once his fame began to spread throughout the surrounding region of Galilee" (Mk. 1:28).
- That same evening after sunset, "the whole city was gathered around the door" (Mk. 1:33).
- The next morning, the disciples found Jesus at prayer, alone in the wilderness. They reported, "Everyone is searching for you" (Mk. 1:37).
- Because the healed leper proclaimed Jesus openly despite Jesus' command to tell no one, "Jesus could no longer go into a town openly" (Mk. 1:45).
- In the setting of the story in which the paralytic is healed, "so many gathered around that there was no longer room for them, not even in front of the door" (Mk. 2:2).
- The people bringing the paralytic "could not bring him to Jesus because of the crowd" and had to dig a hole in the roof (Mk. 2:4).
- After healing the paralytic, Jesus went out beside the sea and "the whole crowd gathered around him" (Mk. 2:13).
- Shortly afterward, many tax collectors and sinners were sitting at table with Jesus in Simon's house "for there were many who followed him" (Mk. 2:15).
- When Jesus departed with his disciples to the sea, "a great multitude from Galilee followed him" (Mk. 3:7).
- Jesus instructed his disciples to get a boat ready "because of the crowd, so that they would not crush him" (Mk. 3:9).
- Mark describes the situation that raised this concern: "All who had diseases pressed upon him to touch him" (Mk. 3:10).
- When Jesus returned home, "the crowd came together again, so that they could not even eat" (Mk. 3:20).
- There at home, Mark portrays the scene: "A crowd was sitting around him" (Mk. 3:32).
- In another scene by the sea, "a great crowd gathered around him" (Mk. 5:21).

- While Jesus is en route to heal the daughter of Jairus, a hemorrhaging woman "came up behind him in the crowd" (Mk. 5:27).
- When Jesus questions who touched him, his disciples note, "You see the crowd pressing in on you" (Mk. 5:31).

This is a brief list of scenes from the early part of Jesus' ministry. Though many of these pericopae have parallels in Matthew's gospel, the Marcan details listed above have systematically been excluded from the Matthean account. Matthew characterizes the "crowd" in a far different way than Mark. They do not speak. They do not hem Jesus in or press up against him. They do not complicate entry into or egress from homes. While they are present, they do not make it difficult for Jesus to enter villages. The crowds in the Matthean narrative are less enthusiastic than their counterparts in Mark.

Like sheep without a shepherd. Not until the end of the third narrative section, near the midpoint of the gospel, is Jesus faced by a crowd large enough that he needs to improvise in order to accommodate them. Matthew reports that "such great crowds gathered around him that he got into a boat and sat there, while the whole crowd stood on the beach" (Mt. 13:2). The context of the scene is significant. Jesus is about to begin the discourse in parables, and the crowd will be Jesus' audience for the parables of the sower (Mt. 13:3–17), weeds (Mt. 13:24–30), mustard seed (Mt. 13:31–32), and yeast (Mt. 13:33).

The parables of the sower and the weeds should be read in light of their narrative context: They are addressed to a large crowd listening to Jesus teach. In the first parable, a sower scatters seed. Though much seed is scattered and many plants begin to grow, only a fraction of the seed will flourish. The parable's explanation offers several reasons why many of the seeds fail to grow to maturity. The first group of failed seed corresponds to the person who hears the word but "does not understand it" (Mt. 13:19). The next group represents one who falls away because "trouble or persecution arises on account of the word" (Mt. 13:21). A third group stands for someone who fails because "the cares of the world and the lure of wealth choke the word" (Mt. 13:22). Matthew makes the explanation of the fruitful seed much more explicit than did Mark; it represents "the one who hears the word and understands it" (Mt. 13:23). Notice that Matthew brackets the parable's explanation with references to "understanding" the word (Mt. 13:19, 23). While a great crowd may be listening to Jesus' teaching, the parable implies that few will understand the word that is taught. The subsequent parable of the weeds amplifies this view. This crowd of would-be disciples contains both wheat and weeds. Many will hear the word, but not all will understand it. A similar message may be inferred from the parable of the net that concludes the discourse in parables.

The parables of the mustard seed and yeast supplement this pessimistic portrait of the crowds. Though only a fraction of people hearing Jesus will understand his word and flourish, that small number who do understand are enough to fulfill the mission. The tiny mustard seed "becomes a tree" large enough for the birds of the air to "make nests in its branches" (Mt. 13:32).[2] A small amount of yeast can leaven three measures of flour (Mt. 13:33).

The crowds in Matthew are thus a mixed bunch. Their words evidence both negative and positive responses to Jesus. As the parables of the sower and wheat suggest, they contain both good and bad. Some in the crowd will prove to be fruitful disciples, while most will fall away. Jesus is characterized as having compassion for the crowd "because they were harassed and helpless, like sheep without a shepherd" (Mt. 9:36). Jesus' compassion for the crowds is a thread that will be found later in the narrative (Mt. 14:14; 15:32; 20:34).

The second narrative section concludes with Jesus saying to the disciples, "The harvest is plentiful, but the laborers are few; therefore ask the Lord of the harvest to send out laborers into his harvest" (Mt. 9:37–38). Immediately thereafter, Jesus prays that the Lord send more workers for the harvest, appoints the Twelve, and delivers his second discourse, the missionary discourse.

Homiletical reflection. Jesus' compassion for the crowds presents an important reminder for today's church. Much preaching comes (appropriately) from a pastoral care model and is addressed to the personal, inward needs of members of our congregations. Many congregations are focused inwardly in their program and worship. Matthew reminds us that faith is not an exclusively inward matter and calls us to attend to the great missional need in the world. When Jesus looks out at the large crowds, he sees not a mass of faceless

---

[2]Compare Mark 4:30–32. The seed becomes "the greatest of shrubs" but not a tree as in Matthew. The birds build nests "in its shade" rather than in its branches as in Matthew.

people but "lost sheep" who are "harassed and helpless." He feels compassion for them and prays for resources to reach them. Matthew's gospel challenges contemporary preachers to put faces on the lost sheep of our world. Can we motivate our congregations to move from compassion to action for the sake of the world's lost sheep?

Matthew's story also encourages us to reconsider the "numbers game" we often play in the church. The media are impressed by megachurches with thousands in attendance and by the member-ship loss of mainline churches. The church often buys into this mentality. Matthew's story deemphasizes the Marcan portrait of Jesus' popularity. The parables of the sower and the weeds remind us that the mission is more than a numbers game. While not unimportant, great crowds do not guarantee that our ministry has been successful. Many may hear the word, but not all will understand it. Some will be unable to withstand trouble or persecution. Others will never move beyond the values of the world, the lure of wealth. The task of evangelism is more than winning converts. The church is called in the great commission to "make disciples,…teaching them to obey everything that I have commanded you" (Mt. 28:19–20). Matthew stresses that our preaching should help our congregations grow to understand their faith.

The Hardships of an Itinerant Missionary

Jesus' mission required more workers for the harvest, and that need continues to face Matthew's church. Workers are scarce precisely because the calling is a costly one. The explanation of the parable of the sower identified several reasons why some seed begins to grow but fails to produce fruit: trouble or persecution, the cares of the world, and the lure of wealth. The missionary discourse names and addresses the costs that must be borne by would-be disciples.

The cares of the world and the lure of wealth. To be in mission re-quires the sacrifice of the normal human pleasures of home and family. The scribe who wants to follow Jesus is warned that "the Son of Man has nowhere to lay his head" (Mt. 8:20). Another dis-ciple who is called to follow Jesus asks for a leave to bury his father; Jesus replies, "Follow me, and let the dead bury their own dead" (Mt. 8:22). Jesus tells the Twelve, "Whoever loves father or mother more than me is not worthy of me; and whoever loves son or daughter more than me is not worthy of me…" (Mt. 10:37). Matthew insists that the calling to "go to the lost sheep of the house of Israel" is the highest priority in the missioner's life, higher even than the relationship to one's parents and children.

Missioners will endure material scarcity. This theme is first introduced in the Sermon on the Mount.

> Therefore I tell you, do not worry about your life, what you will eat or what you will drink, or about your body, what you will wear. Is not life more than food, and the body more than clothing?…Therefore do not worry, saying, "What will we eat?" or "What will we drink?" or "What will we wear?" (Mt. 6:25, 31)

The theme is continued in the missionary discourse. The disciples are instructed, "Take no gold, or silver, or copper in your belts, no bag for your journey, or two tunics, or sandals, or a staff" (Mt. 10:9–10). The narrative relates that "his disciples were hungry" one sabbath and satisfied their hunger by gleaning heads of grain from a grainfield (Mt. 12:1). When Jesus returns to the city the morning after Palm Sunday, he too is described as hungry and frustrated to find no fruit on a fig tree by the side of the road (Mt. 21:18–19). Matthew replies to this challenge, in part, by affirming the blessedness of the poor, of those who hunger and thirst (Mt. 5:3, 10). His gospel encourages disciples to trust in the providence of the heavenly Father who provides the birds of the air with food and clothes the lilies of the field and the grass of the field (Mt. 6:26, 28–30).

At the same time, Matthew understands the disciples' material scarcity to be an instrumental part of the mission. The disciples are to take no provisions for their journey, "for laborers are worthy of their food" (Mt. 10:10, author trans.). The disciples' material neediness sets up a test of hospitality. Being dependent upon the hospitality of those to whom they come, the disciples' first task upon entering a town or village is to "find out who in it is worthy." The worthy are those who welcome the disciples and listen to their words. In every town, the disciples are to accept the hospitality of the worthy, reside with them for the duration of their stay, and give their peace to those homes. Others who refuse to welcome the disciples or to listen to their words will prove themselves unworthy. The disciples are to let the peace they wished upon the unworthy return to them. On leaving an unworthy, inhospitable place, they are to "shake off the dust from your feet as you leave that house or town" as a sign of judgment (Mt. 10:9–15).

This theme reappears in dramatic form in the conclusion of Jesus' final discourse. The parable of the sheep and the goats is set at the end of the age. The Son of Man is seated on his throne. He separates the peoples of all the nations into two groups, the blessed and the accursed. The peoples will be judged on the basis of their response to Jesus or to "the least of his brothers" when they saw them hungry, thirsty, a stranger, naked, sick, or in prison. In other words, the peoples of the world will be judged on the basis of the hospitality offered or refused to those who came in Jesus' name (Mt. 25:31–46).

Matthew offers would-be workers a different perspective by which to understand the material scarcities they will endure. Though he does not deny in any way the reality of the hardships experienced on the mission, those hardships are shown to have a higher purpose. The disciples' suffering will not be meaningless. Their own human neediness will provide the opportunity by which the peoples of the Earth can inherit the kingdom. In the concluding words of the missionary discourse,

> Whoever welcomes you welcomes me, and whoever welcomes me welcomes the one who sent me. Whoever welcomes a prophet in the name of a prophet will receive a prophet's reward; and whoever welcomes a righteous person in the name of a righteous person will receive the reward of the righteous; and whoever gives even a cup of cold water to one of these little ones in the name of a disciple—truly I tell you, none of these will lose their reward. (Mt. 10: 40–42)

Trouble and persecution. Prospective missioners face not only material scarcity but outright persecution. This concern is raised in the birth story. Herod, alarmed at the news that the king of the Jews has been born, searches for the child and seeks to destroy him. Jesus is an object of persecution from the moment of his birth.

The theme of persecution is raised explicitly in the Beatitudes:

Blessed are those who are persecuted
  for righteousness' sake,
for theirs is the kingdom of heaven.
Blessed are you when people revile you
  and persecute you
and utter all kinds of evil against you falsely
  on my account.
Rejoice and be glad, for your reward is great in heaven,
for in the same way they persecuted the prophets
who were before you. (Mt. 5:10–12)

Later in the Sermon on the Mount, Jesus urges his listeners to "pray for those who persecute you" (Mt. 5:44).

The subject is taken up again in the missionary discourse. Jesus warns the Twelve that he is sending them "into the midst of wolves." They will be handed over to councils, flogged in their synagogues, and dragged before governors and kings. The disciples "will be hated by all because of my name." Jesus tells them candidly, "When they persecute you in one town, flee to the next" (Mt. 10:16–23). In the closing apocalyptic discourse, Jesus predicts that the scribes and pharisees will "persecute from town to town" those sent to them (Mt. 23:34, author trans.).

Ultimately, missioners may be brought to trial, where they face the painful alternative of denying Jesus and saving themselves or acknowledging Jesus and enduring the consequences. Again, this issue was raised previously in the Sermon on the Mount. Jesus' followers are the "salt of the earth," and salt that has lost its taste is worthless; they are the "light of the world," and the light is not to be hidden but must be allowed to shine before others (Mt. 5:13–16). In the missionary discourse, Jesus tells the Twelve that when they are handed over and compelled to speak, they are not to worry, "for what you are to say will be given to you at that time; for it is not you who speak, but the Spirit of your Father speaking through you" (Mt. 10:19b–20). Further, they are not to fear those who threaten their physical well-being. The Twelve are encouraged to "tell in the light" what Jesus has told them in the dark, to "proclaim from the housetops" what they have heard whispered. The call is a difficult one, and Jesus does not minimize its challenge. He predicts that some will be unable to remain faithful under persecution and will betray fellow believers to the authorities (Mt. 10:21). Jesus states the consequences of what one does in the time of trial in the strongest possible terms:

> Everyone therefore who acknowledges me before others, I also will acknowledge before my Father in heaven; but whoever denies me before others, I also will deny before my Father in heaven. (Mt. 10:32–33)

Ultimately the Twelve are left with the challenge of taking up the cross. "Those who find their life will lose it, and those who lose their life for my sake will find it" (Mt. 10:39).

Homiletical reflection. Matthew's narrative is directed to a church in which too many members are put off by the hardships of the mission. This problem may sound familiar to contemporary churches, struggling to enlist enough people to teach Sunday school, visit the unchurched, conduct an Every Member Canvas, or even set up for coffee hour. In most churches and voluntary organizations, a small portion of the members do a disproportionate share of the work. How can we encourage the inactive majority to become fruitful disciples?

One of the most moving moments of Matthew's narrative occurs at the conclusion of chapter 9.

> When he saw the crowds, he had compassion for them, because they were harassed and helpless, like sheep without a shepherd. Then he said to his disciples, "The harvest is plentiful, but the laborers are few; therefore ask the Lord of the harvest to send out laborers into his harvest." (Mt. 9: 36–38)

Why is this narrative moment so powerful? Pay attention to Matthew's use of language. He uses words with high emotional impact to describe the crowd: harassed, helpless. He describes Jesus' emotional response to the crowd's situation: compassion. He employs powerful metaphors, inviting readers to consider (a) how the crowds are like (and unlike) sheep without a shepherd and (b) how the work of the mission is like (and unlike) that of a laborer in the harvest. Finally, he uses the language of prayer. Jesus asks the disciples to pray for laborers for the harvest. By praying this prayer, the disciples (1) buy into what Jesus hopes for and (2) visualize the outcome when the Lord provides what has been prayed for.

Matthew's rhetoric offers an important lesson for contemporary preachers. The most persuasive way of eliciting a positive response is to put a human face on the need we want to address. Describing the institution's need for resources ("We are short three Sunday school teachers this year") does not inspire the imagination; institutions always need more resources. Words conveying obligation ("God has given some of you the talent of teaching, and you *ought* to sign up to teach this year") may lead some to respond out of guilt and others to resist an authoritarian message. Instead, tell a story of a child growing up in a troubled home whose life was touched by a compassionate Sunday school teacher...or of a tired and discouraged man who found unexpected joy working with a group of youths.

Put a human face on the missional need. Help your congregation visualize what can happen when God works through our efforts in surprising ways. Speak not only to the mind but to the heart, using words with emotional content. Use metaphors that grab the imagination and continue to speak long after the sermon's content is forgotten.

Understanding the Word

Matthew addresses the shortage of workers for the harvest, a shortage that exists precisely because the task is such a daunting one. Workers in the harvest bear a heavy cross. It involves leaving home and family, facing material scarcity, and facing the possibility of persecution and all its consequences. Many are choosing *not* to carry this cross—the result, in Matthew's analysis, of an inadequate theology of discipleship.

Matthew dramatizes the difference between adequate and inadequate understandings of discipleship. The conclusion of the Sermon on the Mount uses stark contrast to vivify the differences:

- The narrow gate and hard road is contrasted with the wide gate and easy road (Mt. 7:13–14).
- The good tree that bears good fruit is contrasted with the bad tree that bears bad fruit (Mt. 7:17).

- Those who *do* the will of the Father in heaven are contrasted with those who *say*, "Lord, Lord" (Mt. 7:21).
- The wise man who builds his house on rock is contrasted with the foolish man who builds his house on sand (Mt. 7: 24–27).

This same use of stark contrast likewise characterizes the conclusion of Jesus' teaching. The eschatological discourse concludes with three parables:

- Five wise virgins who brought oil for their lamps are contrasted with five foolish virgins who brought no oil (Mt. 25: 1–13).
- Two good and trustworthy slaves who invested their talents and made more are contrasted with the wicked and lazy slave who buried his talent in the ground (Mt. 25:14–30).
- The blessed who cared for the least of Jesus' brothers and sisters when they were in need are contrasted with the accursed who failed to take care of the least of Jesus' family (Mt. 25:31–46).

On legalism. What constitutes an adequate theology of discipleship? Matthew addresses the subject of religious practice. He argues, on the one hand, against legalism. Matthew strongly rejects the notion that either (a) mere external observance of the law or (b) observance of pious acts in order to be seen by others constitutes an adequate discipleship.

The Sermon on the Mount provides a series of illustrations of what Matthew means by mere external observance of the law. Each illustration begins with a variation of the phrase "You have heard that it was said…" (Mt. 5:21, 27, 31, 33, 38, 43). For example, the commandment "You shall not murder" does not speak merely to external behavior. The fulfillment of this commandment involves the human tendency to speak words of violence to people with whom we are angry. Matthew speaks of the need to seek reconciliation with "a brother or sister" who "has something against you" (Mt. 5:21–26). The discourse continues with Matthean interpretations of the law as it concerns adultery (Mt. 5:27–30), divorce (Mt. 5:31–32), false witness (Mt. 5:33–37), limited retaliation for wrongs suffered (Mt. 5:38–42), and loving one's neighbor (Mt. 5:43–48).

The Sermon on the Mount also addresses the subject of ritual observance. Matthew warns against "practicing your piety before others in order to be seen by them" (Mt. 6:1). The discourse addresses specifically the acts of almsgiving, prayer, and fasting. In each case Matthew teaches that these spiritual disciplines be done in secret. Each rhetorical unit concludes with the assurance that "your Father who sees in secret will reward you" (Mt. 6:4, 6, 18).

On antinomianism. Matthew is arguing, at the same time, with those who would say that observing the law or practicing piety is unimportant. Matthew is concerned that there is a pervading antinomianism in the church. Some think that Jesus came to abolish the law. Matthew disagrees pointedly, addressing this contention directly.

> Do not think that I have come to abolish the law or the prophets; I have come not to abolish but to fulfill. For truly I tell you, until heaven and earth pass away, not one letter, not one stroke of a letter, will pass from the law until all is accomplished. Therefore, whoever breaks one of the least of these commandments, and teaches others to do the same, will be called least in the kingdom of heaven; but whoever does them and teaches them will be called great in the kingdom of heaven. For I tell you, unless your righteousness exceeds that of the scribes and Pharisees, you will never enter the kingdom of heaven. (Mt. 5:17–20)

The church had struggled with the role of Jewish law ever since sizable numbers of Gentiles converted to Christianity. Luke-Acts, written roughly at the same time as Matthew, presents one voice in the conversation taking place within the church. Peter's vision revealed that all food is to be considered clean (Acts 10:15). The Jerusalem Conference reduced the law to several essentials, "that you abstain from what has been sacrificed to idols and from blood and from what is strangled and from fornication" (Acts 15:29).[3]

Matthew represents another voice in this conversation. In Matthew's story, Jesus teaches his disciples to keep the commandments and to teach others to do the same. In fact, Jesus' standards of

---

[3]There was no unanimity on the issue of eating food sacrificed to idols. For another voice in the conversation, see 1 Corinthians 8:1–13.

law-keeping are more stringent than those of the scribes and pharisees. External conformity alone will not suffice; true obedience must
come from the heart.

Neither is the law to be relaxed in order to make the faith more
attractive to Gentiles. In the ultimate scene in Matthew's narrative,
the disciples are sent to "make disciples of all nations" (Mt. 28:19).
The Greek noun *ethnos*, translated "nations," also means "Gentiles."
The nations/Gentiles are to be taught "to obey everything that I
have commanded you" (Mt. 28:20). This includes at minimum the
content of the five teaching discourses within the narrative.

Matthew has a profound concern about the widespread disre-
gard for the law within the church. His gospel contains four references
to *anomia* (lawlessness).

(1) At the conclusion of the Sermon on the Mount, Jesus con-
     trasts those who *say* "Lord, Lord" with "the one who does
     the will of my Father in heaven." At the final judgment,
     Jesus will say to the former group, "I never knew you; go
     away from me, you *lawless ones*" (Mt. 7:23, author trans.).

(2) The parable of the weeds describes wheat and weeds grow-
     ing together in the field until the final judgment. In the
     explanation of the parable, Jesus states that at the final judg-
     ment, the angels "will collect out of his kingdom those who
     cause others to sin and the ones who practice *lawlessness*"
     (Mt. 13:41, author trans.).

(3) The eschatological discourse contains a series of six "woes"
     directed at the scribes and pharisees. One of the "woes"
     compares the scribes and pharisees to whitewashed tombs,
     beautiful on the outside but filled with dead bones and filth
     on the inside. "So you also on the outside look righteous to
     others, but inside you are full of hyprocrisy and *lawlessness*"
     (Mt. 23:28).

(4) The eschatological discourse goes on to address those who
     will fall away in the time of persecution. "And because of
     the increase of *lawlessness*, the love of many will grow cold"
     (Mt. 24:12). Matthew offers a corollary to the Pauline no-
     tion that the fulfillment of the law consists of loving one
     another (Rom. 13:8, 10; Gal. 5:14). Lawlessness—disregard
     for the law or disobedience to the law—can lead to

lovelessness, to a heart grown cold. A warm heart that loves both neighbors and enemies cannot develop in a church beset with lawlessness.

The mission has suffered because too many have been put off by the hardships the mission requires. This is the result, in Matthew's analysis, of an inadequate theology of discipleship. Neither legalism nor antinomianism will suffice. True discipleship requires both love and obedience; neither one can exist without the other. While bearing the cross is a costly proposition, Matthew concludes his narrative with the ultimate word of encouragement. Jesus sends his disciples to all the world, knowing the reality of the mission to which he sends them. Yet in his final words, Jesus leaves the disciples—and Matthew leaves his readers—with this assurance: "I am with you always, to the end of the age." Disciples do not go to the mission alone. They go with the authority and constant presence of the one to whom has been given "all authority in heaven and on earth" (Mt. 28:18–20).

Homiletical reflection. Dietrich Bonhoeffer's famous commentary on the Sermon on the Mount, *The Cost of Discipleship*, contrasts "cheap grace" and "costly grace."

> Costly grace is the gospel which must be *sought* again and again, the gift which must be *asked* for, the door at which a man must *knock*. Such grace is *costly* because it calls us to follow, and it is *grace* because it calls us to follow *Jesus Christ*. It is costly because it costs a man his life, and it is grace because it gives a man the only true life. It is costly, because it condemns sin, and grace because it justifies the sinner. Above all, it is *costly* because it cost God the life of his Son...Above all, it is *grace* because God did not reckon his Son too dear a price to pay for our life, but delivered him up for us. Costly grace is the Incarnation of God.[4]

Bonhoeffer originally wrote these words in 1937, in pre–World War II Germany. He was concerned about the direction his country was taking and about the church's acquiescence to the Nazi

---

[4]Dietrich Bonhoeffer, *The Cost of Discipleship*, trans. R. H. Fuller (New York: Macmillan, 1959), 47–48.

movement. Understanding what the gospel required and knowing the risk, Bonhoeffer left the safety of his professorship at Union Theological Seminary in New York. He returned to Germany and became active in the Confessing Church. His faithfulness resulted in his incarceration in a Nazi concentration camp and his execution a few days before the camp was liberated. Bonhoeffer's life offers one of the outstanding portraits of Christian discipleship in the twentieth century.

On the other hand, the acquiescence of the German church to the Nazi movement stands as a haunting reminder to the ages. Because of its inadequate theology of discipleship—"cheap grace" as Bonhoeffer termed it—the church laid aside the authority given by Christ, the one who possesses "all authority in heaven and on earth" (Mt. 28:18). Had the whole church proclaimed the gospel with authority and authenticity, it *could* have changed history. The Nazi atrocities could never have been committed had the church as a whole called for justice and resisted evil.

The church possesses the authority of Christ and is called to make disciples of all nations, but it has squandered that authority, both in Matthew's day and in our own. Matthew continues to challenge the church. If we hear and understand the word, if we dare to speak of God's grace and judgment, we will influence the world with the word of God.

Seeking Healing and Renewal in the Church

Matthew has addressed his narrative to a church in which too many have been dissuaded by the hardships required by the mission. He has tried to correct the inadequate understanding of discipleship conveyed by many teachers in the church. At the same time, Matthew recognizes that divisions of doctrine and practice within the church compromise its integrity and impair its mission. It is inappropriate—not to mention counterproductive—to bask in one's own righteousness while despising those who have gone astray. After all, one's place in the kingdom depends upon God's mercy, not upon one's own righteousness.

The Sermon on the Mount introduces a number of issues having to do with problems that inevitably occur in the life of any community. The fourth of the five discourses in Matthew's narrative, the community discourse, addresses these problems in some depth. The Matthean response can be summarized under the rubric "judge not, that you be not judged" (Mt. 7:1, RSV).

On mercy. The Beatitudes encourage Christian disciples to be merciful (Mt. 5:7). It is productive to pursue the narrative thread of "mercy" throughout Matthew's story. On two occasions, Jesus will quote Hosea 6:6 to the pharisees: "I desire mercy and not sacrifice" (Mt. 9:13; 12:7). The pharisees have criticized Jesus for eating with tax collectors and sinners and condemned the disciples for plucking and eating grain on the Sabbath. Jesus tells them, in the first instance, to "go and learn what this means" (9:13) and, in the second, tells them that "if you had known what this means…you would not have condemned the guiltless." On another occasion, Jesus criticizes the scribes and pharisees. While they have practiced tithing, they have "neglected the weightier matters of the law: justice and mercy and faith" (Mt. 23:23).

There are four occasions in Matthew's narrative on which characters ask Jesus for healing. Two blind men receive their sight (Mt. 9:27–30). A Canaanite woman asks Jesus to exorcise the demon from her daughter (Mt. 15:22–28). A father asks Jesus to heal his son's epilepsy (Mt. 17:14–18). Again, two blind men receive their sight (Mt. 20:29–34). In each case, they ask Jesus, "Have mercy on me/us."[5] In these four stories, Matthew characterizes Jesus as consistently responding to pleas for mercy. Jesus is merciful, and he heals the afflicted as acts of mercy.

Matthew seeks to promote the quality of mercy within the church family. The community discourse concludes with the parable of the unmerciful servant. A slave owes the king a debt of ten thousand talents, an amount beyond imagination. The slave begs the king's forgiveness, and the king forgives this debt. This same slave encounters a fellow slave who owes him a hundred denarii.[6] The

---

[5]Matthew's narrative differs significantly from Mark's. In Mark, only blind Bartimaeus says, "Have mercy on me" (Mk. 10:47, 48). Matthew has split the Bartimaeus pericope into twin pericopae; in each pericope two blind men ask for mercy and receive their sight. Mark does not characterize the Canaanite woman (Mk. 7:26) or the boy's father (Mk. 9:17–18) as asking Jesus "to have mercy" on their children.

[6]One denarius was a day's wage for a common laborer, and one talent is equivalent in value to 6,000 denarii. Accordingly the first slave is forgiven a debt of 60 million days' wages and refuses to forgive his fellow slave a debt of 100 days' wages. See John W. Betlyon, "Coinage," *Anchor Bible Dictionary,* ed. David Noel Freedman (Garden City, N.Y.: Doubleday, 1992), 1:1086, and Marvin A. Powell, "Weights and Measures," *Anchor Bible Dictionary,* 6:908.

fellow slave begs forgiveness, using precisely the same words that the first slave used in begging forgiveness of the king, but the plea for forgiveness is ignored. The slave has the debtor thrown into prison. The king has the final word to the slave: "Should you not have had mercy on your fellow slave, as I had mercy on you?" (Mt. 18:33).

On forgiveness. As the parable of the unmerciful servant suggests, the capacity to offer forgiveness is essential for life in community. Matthew develops this theme in his narrative. The model prayer that Jesus uses to teach his disciples how to pray (the Lord's Prayer) includes the petition "And forgive us our debts, as we also have forgiven our debtors." At the immediate conclusion of the prayer Jesus offers this commentary: "For if you forgive others their trespasses, your heavenly Father will also forgive you; but if you do not forgive others, neither will your Father forgive your trespasses" (Mt. 6:12, 14–15).

The community discourse expands on the practice of forgiveness. Quite specific instructions are given in the event that "another member of the church sins against you." The injured party is first to meet alone with the offending member of the church. If this fails, there is to be a further effort with one or two others. Finally, the matter is to be brought before the entire church. Only if all of these efforts fails is that member to be written off. The motivation is to "regain" that member, to seek reconciliation (Mt. 18:15–17).

The community discourse also addresses the limits of forgiveness. Peter asks, "If another member of the church sins against me, how often should I forgive? As many as seven times?" (Mt. 18:21). Luke's gospel says, simply, "And if the same person sins against you seven times a day, and turns back to you seven times and says, 'I repent,' you must forgive" (Lk. 17:4). Matthew expands the scope of forgiveness considerably. One is to forgive, depending on how one translates the Greek, "seventy-seven" (NRSV) or "seventy times seven" (RSV) times (Mt. 18:22).

The community discourse concludes with the parable of the unmerciful servant, which I have discussed above. The parable concludes with the master punishing the forgiven slave who would not show mercy to his fellow slave. Jesus offers a one-sentence commentary on the story: "So my heavenly Father will also do to every one of you, if you do not forgive your brother or sister from your heart" (Mt. 18:35).

Matthew's readers are to be willing to extend forgiveness to those who have sinned against them. However, forgiveness must be exercised in both directions. Matthew's readers need to be willing to ask forgiveness from those whom they may have offended. "So when you are offering your gift at the altar, if you remember that your brother or sister has something against you, leave your gift there before the altar and go; first be reconciled to your brother or sister, and then come and offer your gift" (Mt. 5:23–24).

On those who have gone astray. There are false prophets in the church (Mt. 7:15; 24:11, 24), and Jesus warns that many in the church will be deceived by them (Mt. 18:12–13; 24:4–5, 11, 24).[7] The community discourse introduces the parable of the lost sheep with the instruction, "Take care that you do not despise one of these little ones" (Mt. 18:10). The parable goes on to talk about a shepherd who has a hundred sheep, one of which has "gone astray" (so the NRSV) or, literally, "has been deceived." The shepherd's mission is to go after the one that has been deceived. "And if he finds it, truly I tell you, he rejoices over it more than over the ninety-nine that never went astray" (Mt. 18:13).

Matthew seems concerned that some in the church, in their judgmentalism, are too quick to write off those who have been deceived. Two parables in the discourse on parables, the parables of the wheat (Mt. 13:24–30) and the net (Mt. 13:47–50), deserve special attention in this context. In the first parable, a field is sowed with wheat, but when the plants appear, the field is a mixture of wheat and weeds. In the second parable, a net is cast into the sea and is pulled back in filled with both good and bad fish. These parables describe the situation of Matthew's church, a church that is filled with both productive and nonproductive disciples, some who have remained faithful while others have gone astray, some who are entering the narrow gate into the hard way while others are choosing the wide gate into the easy way, some who are building their house on rock while others build on sand.

The instinctive response of many in the church—to rid the church of these inadequate disciples—is represented by the householder's slaves. They offer to go into the wheat field and gather the weeds. The householder's response surprises them: "No; for in

---

[7]The Greek verb *planao*, sometimes translated "led astray," literally means "deceived."

gathering the weeds you would uproot the wheat along with them. Let both of them grow together until the harvest..." (Mt. 13:29–30). Human beings, no matter how well intentioned, will make mistakes in judgment. Some true disciples would inadvertently be excommunicated, while presumably some false disciples would be missed in the purge. Thus, Jesus tells his disciples, "Do not judge, so that you may not be judged...You hypocrite, first take the log out of your own eye, and then you will see clearly to take the speck out of your neighbor's eye" (Mt. 7:1, 5).

Homiletical reflection. In Matthew's day as in our day, it is not simply the case that the church is a mixture of saints and sinners. It also needs to be said that even saints are sinners. Matthew calls Christians to practice mercy, never forgetting that we have a place in the kingdom only because we have received God's mercy. The calling is to seek out the "little ones" who have been deceived, suspending judgment and offering forgiveness with a heart full of mercy. "Blessed are the merciful," Jesus reminds us, "for they will receive mercy" (Mt. 5:7).

Responding to Opponents beyond the Church

Matthew's story of Jesus describes a narrative world that is highly conflicted. The plot is, from the beginning, highly charged with tension. Jesus' birth is a cosmic event marked by the appearance of a new star in the heavens. Seeing the star, astrologers from the East come to Jerusalem seeking "the child who has been born king of the Jews." Hearing this news, King Herod becomes "frightened, and all Jerusalem with him," consults the chief priests and scribes "where the Messiah was to be born," and acquires the information necessary to eliminate this mutual threat (Mt. 2:2–5). Herod seeks to destroy the child, but his intentions are foiled. Both the astrologers and Joseph heed the message they receive in a dream, and the infant Jesus is saved from this attempt on his life.

In Matthew's narrative, Jesus' life is thus conflicted from his birth.[8] The protagonist and antagonists are established from the narrative's beginning. Characters are clearly identified either as allies or enemies of Jesus. Herod and the people of Jerusalem are characterized

---

[8]Realize how different this is from the other synoptic accounts: Mark's has no birth narrative, and Luke's concludes with the notation that Jesus increased "in divine and human favor" (Lk. 2:52).

as being troubled by the birth of the protagonist. The chief priests and scribes cooperate with Herod, providing information that he will use to seek Jesus' death. Joseph and the astrologers are Jesus' allies who save him from an untimely death. They are characterized as heeding the word that comes to them in dreams through the angel of the Lord.

Matthew's ending reinforces the narrative tension. As was his birth, Jesus' death is described as a cosmic event. As in Mark, darkness came upon all the earth from noon until three o'clock, and the curtain of the temple was torn. The Matthean narrative, however, also describes an earthquake and a general resurrection of saints who had died (Mt. 27:51–53). Later in the narrative, as Mary Magdalene and the other Mary go to see the tomb, there is another earthquake (an aftershock?) and the stone that sealed the tomb is rolled away (Mt. 28:1–2).[9]

It is interesting to notice that Matthew creates a literary sandwich, placing the account of the empty tomb (Mt. 28:1–10) within a story in which the major characters are the chief priests and the guards at the tomb (Mt. 27:62–66; 28:11–15). This use of a literary sandwich (intercalation) invites the reader to read and interpret these two stories together. The chief priests and pharisees go to Pilate the day after Jesus is buried. They have heard that Jesus (whom they call an "imposter," or literally, "the deceitful one") had said, "After three days I will rise again." They are concerned that Jesus' disciples will steal his body from the tomb and claim, "He has been raised from the dead." Were this to happen, "the last deception would be worse than the first."

Following the events at the empty tomb, the guards tell the chief priests "everything that had happened." Ironically the guards are the first bearers of the Easter message in Matthew's story, and the chief priests are the first to hear the news (although I doubt Matthew intended this irony). Hearing the guards' report, Matthew characterizes the chief priests as inventing a counternarrative.

They bribe the guards and instruct them, "You must say, 'His disciples came by night and stole him away while we were asleep.'"

---

[9]Earlier in the story, it was an earthquake that caused the boat in which Jesus and the disciples were crossing the sea to become swamped (Mt. 8:24). In the eschatological discourse, earthquakes are described as the "birthpangs" of Jesus'"coming and of the end of the age" (Mt. 24:8, 3). This is an interesting narrative thread that merits further investigation.

They do as they are instructed. At this point, Matthew speaks directly to the implied reader: "And this story is still told among the Jews to this day."

This story exposes the opposition that Matthew's church is facing. There are two competing narratives concerning Jesus. According to the church's narrative, Jesus was raised. According to the narrative told among the Jews, Jesus' body was stolen from the tomb. There are also countercharges of deception. The chief priests called Jesus "that deceiver" and worried that the disciples would steal his body and perpetrate "the last deception," the story of his resurrection. Matthew, in turn, characterizes the chief priests as knowing the truth yet inventing a lie that has deceived many.

Consider, too, Jesus' concern that his followers guard against deception. In the parable of the lost sheep, "a shepherd has a hundred sheep, and one of them was deceived." If the shepherd recovers it, "he rejoices over it more than over the ninety-nine that never were deceived" (Mt. 18:12, 13, author trans.). The eschatological discourse contains a number of warnings to guard against deception. Note that the Greek verb *planao*, often translated "to lead astray," is the same verb used in Matthew 27:63–64.

- Beware that no one deceives you (Mt. 24:4, author trans.).
- For many will come in my name, saying, "I am the Messiah!" and they will deceive many (Mt. 24:5, author trans.).
- And many false prophets will arise and deceive many (Mt. 24:11, author trans.).
- For false messiahs and false prophets will appear and produce great signs and omens, to deceive, if possible, even the elect (Mt. 24:24, author trans.).

Matthew's narrative addresses a context in which believers and potential believers must decide *whose* story is true, *whose* narrative is more credible. He characterizes the chief priests as deceivers who know the truth yet choose to perpetrate a lie. At the beginning of the narrative, they are the first to know where the Messiah would be born (Mt. 2:4–5). At the end of the narrative, they are the first to hear the news of the resurrection.

Homiletical reflection. Contemporary readers of the gospel of Matthew need to examine critically the implied author's use of rhetoric.[10] He derogates his opponents. His protagonist calls them hypocrites (Mt. 23:13, 15, 23, 25, 27, 29). He characterizes them as liars. Matthew's gospel has been used by some to justify anti-Jewish sentiment and action. I want to assert unequivocally that such anti-Judaism is utterly inappropriate to the gospel. We can observe that the implied author does not always practice the ethic professed by Jesus, when Jesus says, "But I say to you, Love your enemies and pray for those who persecute you, so that you may be children of your Father in heaven" (Mt. 5:44–45).

Preaching Matthew's Gospel

When we preachers have told the story of Peter's confession, it is more than likely that we have had Matthew's version in mind. It is by far the longest and most elaborate of the three tellings of the confession. Only in Matthew does Peter go on to call Jesus "the son of the living God." Only in Matthew does Jesus congratulate Peter on his insight: "Blessed are you, Simon son of Jonah! For flesh and blood has not revealed this to you, but my Father in heaven." Only in Matthew does the confession become the occasion on which Simon receives the name *Peter* and on which Jesus declares "on this rock I will build my church."

Our traditional practice in the church has been to combine the details of the three synoptics into one harmonized account of the life of Jesus. This book has urged preachers to reconsider this practice. The particular way Mark told the story is important if we are to understand Mark's theological way of addressing the church and its situation. The same is true of Luke's confession story and the meaning of Luke–Acts. Our task now is to explore that most familiar of the confession pericopae, Matthew's version.

Often a text's familiarity gets in the way of its being able to speak to us anew. Reading the confession in light of the entire

---

[10]It may or may not be fair to speak of a single historical author who wrote this story. We can only speculate about the historical process by which the narrative was actually constructed—that is, the role of sources and the redactional decisions that may have been made. I am really speaking of the narrative's "implied author," the creative force implied by the sum of the decisions made in the creation of the final text.

Matthean narrative offers one way to move beyond the problem of over-familiarity. How does this text contribute to the whole of Matthew's story, and how does Matthew's story-as-a-whole shed new light on the account of Peter's confession?

Brainstorming and Researching the Gospel

Redaction criticism—comparing one version of a pericope with its parallels—offers a helpful way to begin an exploration. What becomes immediately apparent is that Matthew's confession *adds* much distinctive content to the Marcan original; Luke's confession pericope was considerably *shorter* than Mark's. Matthew's confession contains an extended block of material that is unique to the first gospel. After identifying Jesus as the Messiah, Peter goes on to call him

> "the Son of the living God." And Jesus answered him,
> "Blessed are you, Simon son of Jonah! For flesh and blood
> has not revealed this to you, but my Father in heaven. And
> I tell you, you are Peter, and on this rock I will build my
> church, and the gates of Hades will not prevail against it. I
> will give you the keys of the kingdom of heaven, and what-
> ever you bind on earth will be bound in heaven, and what-
> ever you loose on earth will be loosed in heaven."
> (Mt. 16:16b–19)

This block of material represents a fertile beginning place for ex-ploring narrative links with Matthew's larger story.

Competing claims of authority. "You are Peter, and upon this rock I will build my church." Peter is here vested with considerable authority because his confession is correct. Thus, christological orthodoxy—knowing and confessing Jesus as Messiah and Son of God—is a criterion in Matthew's narrative world for determining who truly possesses authority. The thread of authority runs through the Matthean narrative. In the face of competing claims of authority, who truly speaks, teaches, and acts on behalf of God? This is at the heart of the conflict between the narrative's protagonist and antagonists.

- Both Jesus and the scribes teach the law, but only Jesus' teaching is characterized as authoritative. At the conclusion of the
  Sermon on the Mount, the narrator asserts that Jesus taught
  the crowds "as one having authority, and not as their scribes."

In evidence of this assertion, the crowds are characterized as being "astounded" at Jesus' teaching (Mt. 7:28–29).

- A Roman centurion, a military officer presumably familiar with the aura of authority, recognizes that Jesus possesses authority (Mt. 8:8–9).
- When Jesus forgives the sins of the paralyzed man, the scribes describe that action as blasphemous. Jesus asserts that he possesses "authority on earth" to forgive sins. The ensuing story offers evidence of this authority as Jesus performs the more extraordinary action of commanding the paralyzed man to walk. The crowds again are characterized as responding with awe that "God...had given such authority to human beings" (Mt. 9:2–8).
- In Matthew's narrative world, authority is either "from heaven" or "of human origin." When Jesus heals the blind and the lame in the temple, the chief priests and elders of the people confront him: "By what authority are you doing these things, and who gave you this authority?" Jesus in turn confronts his questioners with the origin of John's baptism; they refuse to answer (Mt. 21:23–27). In Matthew's narrative world, one side possesses authentic authority and the other side is a pretender.
- The narrative concludes with Jesus' ultimate assertion of his own authority: "All authority in heaven and on earth has been given to me" (Mt. 28:18).

Hidden and revealed. Jesus tells Peter, "Flesh and blood has not revealed this to you, but my Father in heaven" (Mt. 16:17). There are competing *claims* of authority in Matthew's narrative world (and in the real context of Matthew's readers). Of all the human characters in the narrative, Peter is said to possess authentic authority. Peter confesses Jesus as Messiah and Son of God because God has *chosen* to reveal truth to Peter. Truth is hidden and cannot be known by mere human discernment. It can be known only through divine revelation.

Matthew's narrative develops this thread of the hidden nature of divine truth.

- Jesus says to the disciples in the missionary discourse, "Nothing is *covered* that will not be revealed, or *hidden* that will not be known" (Mt. 10:26, RSV).

- Jesus thanks the Father in a prayer "because you have *hidden* these things from the wise and intelligent and have revealed them to infants…no one knows the Son except the Father, and no one knows the Father except the Son and anyone to whom the Son chooses to reveal him" (Mt. 11:25, 27b).
- Jesus comments on his own use of parables: "I will open my mouth to speak in parables; I will proclaim what has been *hidden* from the foundation of the world" (Mt. 13:35).
- The thread of hiddenness is woven explicitly into two parables in the discourse. "The kingdom of heaven is like yeast that a woman took and *hid* in three measures of flour until all of it was leavened" (Mt. 13:33, RSV). Again, "the kingdom of heaven is like a treasure *hidden* in a field, which someone found and *hid*; then in his joy he goes and sells all that he has and buys that field" (Mt. 13:44).

Peter is the recipient of divine revelation; he has been given the hidden truth of the kingdom of heaven. He knows that Jesus is not only the Messiah but "Son of the living God." This is, for Matthew, the imprimatur that Peter possesses authentic authority as a teacher in the church.

Built on the rock. In Matthew's telling of the story, Simon receives a new name in the aftermath of the confession: "You are Peter." Peter is entrusted with a foundational role in the church; Jesus will *build* his church on the "*rock*"; this saying plays on the fact that the name Peter (Petros) and the Greek word for rock (petra) are based on the same root. Jesus promises that the church built on a rock will prevail against the gates of Hades; in other words, it will withstand opposition.

There are strong narrative links between the Matthean confession and the parable that concludes the Sermon on the Mount.

Everyone then who hears these words of mine and acts on them will be like a wise man who built his house on rock. The rain fell, the floods came, and the winds blew and beat on that house, but it did not fall, because it had been founded on rock. And everyone who hears these words of mine and does not act on them will be like a foolish man who built his house on sand. The rain fell, and the floods came, and the winds blew and beat against that house, and it fell—and great was its fall! (Mt. 7:24–27)

First, both pericopae speak of *building* a house or church. The same Greek verb (*oikodomeo*, to build) is used in both the parable and the confession. Second, in both passages, the house or church is built on rock (*petra*). Third, in both pericopae, Jesus states that the edifice will withstand forces that can potentially destroy it. The church will prevail against the gates of Hades; the house will withstand rain, floods, and winds.

What is the relationship of house (*oikia*) and church (*ecclesia*)? While the term *church* is used extensively in Acts and the rest of the New Testament, it is used rarely in the gospels; *ecclesia* occurs in only two places, both in Matthew's gospel (Mt. 16:18; 18:17). The term *house* is used frequently in the synoptics and may be a theological metaphor representing "the center of economic and political life as well as religious and ecclesial life."[11]

The power to bind and loose. The power to bind and loose represents the authority to determine "what the law allows and forbids."[12] The authority Peter is given in the church is comparable to the power the Supreme Court has in our county, to interpret the Constitution. Authority is given to Peter in Matthew 16:19 to "bind and loose." This same authority is given to the disciples at large in the community discourse. "Truly I tell you, whatever you *bind* on earth will be *bound* in heaven, and whatever you *loose* on earth will be *loosed* in heaven" (Mt. 18:18).

However, with this authority Jesus provides the disciples with a legal hermeneutic. The disciples are to teach *obedience* both to the law and to Jesus' teachings.

- Jesus says in the Sermon on the Mount, "Whoever does [the least of these commandments] and teaches them will be called great in the kingdom of heaven" (Mt. 5:19).
- In the great commission, Jesus directs the disciples to teach the baptized "to obey everything that I have commanded you" (Mt. 28:20).

Although the disciples are given authority to "loose," Matthew's conservative stance discourages a libertarian approach to the law.

---

[11]Michael H. Crosby, *House of Disciples: Church, Economics, and Justice in Matthew* (Maryknoll, N.Y.: Orbis Books, 1988), 11.

[12]Mark Allan Powell, *God With Us: A Pastoral Theology of Matthew's Gospel* (Minneapolis: Fortress Press, 1995), 22, n. 36.

"Whoever *looses* one of the least of these commandments, and teaches others to do the same, will be called least in the kingdom of heaven" (Mt. 5:19, author trans.). Matthew's narrative warns its readers not to trust all within the church who purport to speak with authority. Jesus warns of "false prophets" (Mt. 7:15) and is explicit that "many" who address Jesus as "Lord, Lord" and perform deeds of power in Jesus' name will not enter the kingdom of heaven (Mt. 7:21–23). In Matthew's narrative world, not everyone who teaches in the name of Jesus possesses Jesus' imprimatur. The authority to teach in Jesus' name is given in this narrative to Peter and to the ten remaining disciples.

Establishing the Sermon's Plotline

Typically, preachers introduce the sermon's text at the beginning of the message. The text is used to raise a question, to upset the equilibrium. Sometimes, however, we have before us a text that offers an answer, a definitive word. Such is the case in my reading of Peter's confession in its Matthean context. Thus, I will use *another* Matthean text—discovered in the process of brainstorming narrative links to the confession—to create disequilibrium in the sermon's beginning. The confession will be introduced later in the sermon to provide the sermon's clue to resolution.

Disequilibrium. At the conclusion of the Sermon on the Mount is a brief parable contrasting the wise man who built a house on rock with the foolish man who build a house on sand (Mt. 7:24–27). There is much in this text that can be exploited to upset the equilibrium. There is conflict in the contrast between the characters in the parable itself; one is wise and the other is foolish. There is conflict in the content of this brief narrative; the rain, floods, and winds threaten the houses that the two characters have built.

Even more intriguing, however, is the foolishness of someone who would build a house on *sand.* While this behavior defies common sense, Matthew uses it to dramatize his rhetorical purposes. He is concerned that the church of his day suffers from the inadequate understanding of Christian discipleship that some leaders within the church are promoting. Those who follow such teaching are building on sand, metaphorically speaking. This observation raises an inescapable question: What does it mean to build on rock?

Resolution. I will use the confession to resolve this question. Peter acclaims Jesus as "the Messiah, the Son of the living God." Jesus responds, "You are Peter, and *on this rock I will build my church.*" In my reading of the confession, the "rock" refers to Peter's christological affirmation. I will expand the christological material by weaving in another narrative link running through Matthew; the gospel begins with a reference to Jesus as "Emmanuel…which means, 'God is with us'" (Mt. 1:23). The gospel concludes with words that echo the narrative's beginning: "I am with you" (Mt. 28:20).[13]

The parable raised a disturbing image—the potentially devastating impact of "rain, floods, and winds." I will also use the confession to resolve this disequilibrium. Just as houses built on rock can withstand such natural forces, Jesus promises that the church he will build on rock will prevail against "the gates of Hades."

Being Open to Contemporary Images

The biblical material offers two kinds of images. The first concerns ground on which a house is built: either sand or rock. The second concerns forces that assail the structural integrity of that house: rain, floods, and winds. The sermon will offer two contemporary images that convey these themes.

(a) The Loma Prieta earthquake. Memories of Loma Prieta would be very present to a congregation in the San Francisco Bay Area. I will use images of the damage caused by this earthquake—especially the devastation wrought in the Marina District of San Francisco—to dramatize the significance of the kind of ground on which a building is constructed. As the intended audience is extremely conscious of earthquake preparedness, this image has the potential to engage the congregation's attention in a powerful way.

(b) Social controversies. The biblical material addresses theological and ethical threats to the church by using the metaphor of natural forces that threaten a house. The sermon will address the fact of social controversies that threaten to divide the church of today. I will introduce images that speak

---

[13]David R. Bauer points out this feature of the structure of Matthew's gospel. See *The Structure of Matthew's Gospel: A Study in Literary Design,* Journal for the Study of the New Testament Supplements 31 (Sheffield: Almond, 1988), 109–34.

to the deep divide between conservatives and liberals in our society by naming some of those wedge issues: abortion, same-sex unions, gun control, taxes, welfare, and health care. The sermon will not take a stance on these issues; its point is to address the destructive influence of such issues on a church not founded on "rock."

Weaving the Sermon

The sermon's plotline uses the narrative thread that connects Peter's confession and the parable of the wise and the foolish men. Woven into that plot are two contemporary threads I have just identified. I will also use three additional threads from the Matthean narrative. First, Matthew highlights the seriousness of the church's inadequate understanding of discipleship with a series of pericopae that contrast would-be disciples from true disciples. Second, Matthew seeks healing and renewal in the church by stressing an ethic of love, forgiveness, and mercy. Finally, Matthew affirms Jesus' unique relationship with God.

❖

How Firm a Foundation
Matthew 16:13–20

Everyone who hears these words of mine and acts on them
    will be like a wise man who built his house on rock.
The rain fell, the floods came,
    and the winds blew and beat on that house,
but it did not fall, because it had been founded on rock.
And everyone who hears these words of mine
  and does not act on them
    will be like a foolish man who built his house on sand.
The rain fell, and the floods came,
    and the winds blew and beat against that house,
and it fell—and great was its fall!

It makes a difference what we build on.
    A house built on rock
    will withstand the forces of nature.
    A house built on sand will deteriorate over time.

It seems so perfectly obvious, yet people do build on sand.
Nineteen eighty-nine was the year of the Loma Prieta
   earthquake.
Striking just hours before game three of the World Series
      between the Oakland A's and the San Francisco Giants,
Loma Prieta did major damage to the Bay Area.
A section of the upper deck of the Bay Bridge collapsed.
The Cypress and Embarcadero freeways
   suffered major damage.
Candlestick Park needed repairs, delaying the series.
But there's one image I remember most vividly of all.
The horrible scene was played over and over
   on the television news:
      flashing red lights from emergency vehicles
        in front of burning fires and collapsed townhouses
          in the Marina District in San Francisco.
Why did such devastation strike there?
Because of the ground on which those houses were built...
   they were built on fill.
The earth shook, the fill liquefied, and disaster occurred.
Gas mains ruptured. Fires broke out.
   Buildings fell off their foundations.
This is no great mystery.
If you build a house on sand, near an active fault,
   what do you think will happen?

Matthew wasn't so much worried about San Francisco real
   estate.
Matthew was concerned about the kind of foundation
   that the church of his day was building on.
Words of warning echo through his gospel...
• About five foolish bridesmaids
   who neglected to bring oil for their lamps...
      They found themselves locked out
      of the wedding banquet
        and heard the bridegroom say, "I do not know you."
• The same thing will be heard by would-be disciples
   who call Jesus "Lord, Lord" with their lips,
      but not with their deeds...

and Jesus will say, "I never knew you."
- Matthew warns about countless people
  who enter wide, inviting gates
    and travel easy, attractive roads…
    that lead to destruction.
Matthew is concerned about a church
  that is building on sand,
    a church that has lost sight of its foundation:
    faith and ethics together—
      What do we believe?
      and how do we live out that faith?

Faith and ethics together…
Ethics has to do with how we live out our faith,
    and Matthew's gospel gets really specific about ethics.
If we believe in a God who loves us,
  forgives us, and shows mercy to us,
    then we live out that faith
      by loving and forgiving
        and showing mercy to others.
- God loves even those who are enemies,
  who need to be reconciled,
    and so are we called to love
    not only neighbors but enemies:
      It was said to folks of old,
      love your neighbor and hate your enemy,
      but I say to you, love your enemy
      and pray for those who persecute you.
- God forgives us completely when we ask forgiveness,
    and so are we called to practice forgiveness:
      How many times, Peter asked, must I forgive
        another member of the church
          who sins against me?
      In Luke's gospel, the answer is "seven times."
      In Matthew… "seventy times seven."
- God has been merciful to us,
    God's steadfast love endures forever,
      and while it's human nature
        for religious people to judge others,

Matthew calls us beyond judgment to mercy:
> Blessed are the merciful, we hear in the Beatitudes,
> for they shall receive mercy.

An ethic of love, forgiveness, and mercy
> is part of the foundation…
>> but that ethic
>> apart from the faith in which it is grounded
>>> is but a foundation of sand
>>>> that will wash away in the storms of life.

The ethic of how we live is grounded in our faith,
> in what we believe.

In Matthew's story, that faith is built
> on the mystery of incarnation.

Remember how the story begins?
The angel spoke a promise to Joseph:
> Look, the virgin shall conceive and bear a son,
> and they shall name him Emmanuel,
> which means, "God is with us."

Remember how the story ends?
Jesus' final words carried echoes of the angel's promise:
> And remember, I am with you always…

God is with us.
I am with you.
At the center of the story,
> the disciples find themselves in Caesarea Philippi.

Jesus asks them the question of questions:
> Who do you say that I am?

Peter speaks the truth:
> You are the Messiah, the Son of the living God.

And Jesus confirms that answer:
> Upon this rock I will build my church.

This is foundational stuff.
This is the rock upon which wise women and men
> will build their homes.

Our faith is grounded in the mystery…
> Jesus is the Messiah, the Son of the living God.
> God-with-us.

This is the bedrock of Christian faith.

And the rains will fall, and the floods will come,
and the winds will blow and beat against that house…
Just like Matthew's church,
today's church is facing rains and floods
and winds of adversity.
Social controversies are tearing at the fabric of our society,
and those same controversies are tearing
at the unity of our church.
We struggle with important ethical questions:
• On abortion, some are pro-life.
Others are pro-choice.
• Some are sympathetic to same-sex unions.
To others, they violate the moral fabric of society.
• Some see the welfare system as a snare
that entraps rather than empowers
those it tries to help.
Others see it as an essential safety net.
On these and dozens of other issues…
from taxes to social security to medical care
our society—and our church—
are being torn by voices from the extremes.
The contrast between the right and the left is so stark,
and few are the voices
that are trying to meet at the center,
to reason together.
The conflict is polarizing our society
and tearing apart our church.
The body of Christ is facing schism.
The rains and the floods and the winds are beating against
our house.
What are we building on?

Wise folk build houses on rock.
If we know what we believe
but do not live out our faith
or make our social witness,
we're foolish disciples who say "Lord, Lord"
but fail to do God's will.

But likewise,
when social positions become our defining issues,
    as they have all across the church,
we are foolishly building on sand.

Wise folk build houses on rock.
Matthew would call us back to that firm foundation.
Matthew would call us back to the mystery
    of the God who loves and forgives and is merciful to us
    and to the challenge of loving others
    with the love we have known.
Matthew would call us back to the mystery
    of God made incarnate in Jesus,
    the Messiah, the Son of the living God,
    God-with-us,
and to the challenge of making God incarnate in the world.
This is the mystery of our faith,
    that undergirds the challenge of living it out.
This is the bedrock on which wise disciples build.
And the rains may fall,
    and the floods may come,
        and the winds may blow,
            and the earth may shake,
                but the house will not fall.
We may even confront the gates of Hades themselves,
    but neither shall these powers prevail against us
        if our house is built on rock.
"You are the Messiah," Peter said,
    "the Son of the living God."
"You are Peter," said Jesus,
    "and on that rock I will build my church."

Reflection on the Sermon

It makes a difference what we build on. The sermon uses the text (Peter's confession) not to upset the equilibrium but to provide the clue to resolution. Therefore I begin the sermon with another narrative moment from Matthew's gospel. I use the parable of the wise and foolish men from the Sermon on the Mount to upset the equilibrium. The parable puts forth the image of rain, floods, and winds assailing the two houses and dramatizes the foolishness of someone who would build a house on sand. I juxtapose a series of contemporary images from the 1989 Loma Prieta earthquake, concluding the series by reminding the congregation of a familiar televised image—fires burning in front of townhouses that collapsed because they were built on fill.

Matthew wasn't so much worried about San Francisco real estate. Residents of the Bay Area, the intended audience for this sermon, are extremely conscious of earthquakes. They would relate naturally to the idea that building on sand is foolish. I use this natural identification to move to a discussion of the deeper issues that Matthew is addressing. I introduce a thread of Matthean passages that contrast the behavior of wise and foolish persons. While the wise bridesmaids are welcomed to the wedding banquet, the foolish bridesmaids who neglected to bring oil for their lamps are turned away with the words "I do not know you" (Mt. 25:1–13). Jesus warns that not all who *say* "Lord, Lord" will enter the kingdom; unless would-be disciples also *do* the will of his father, they will hear "I never knew you" at the judgment (Mt. 7:21–23). I conclude the thread with Jesus' metaphor contrasting the narrow gate and the hard road that leads to life with the wide gate and the easy road that leads to destruction (Mt. 7:13–14).

This thread develops the disequilibrium. It relates the collapse of the house built on sand (and townhouses built on fill) to Christian discipleship. I highlight Matthew's warning: Judgment awaits would-be disciples who fail to build their discipleship on an adequate foundation. This section of the sermon concludes by raising two questions that will occupy the remainder of the sermon, faith and ethics.

Faith and ethics together. My overall rhetorical strategy for the sermon determined the decision to begin with the question of ethics. I want to withhold revealing the sermon's "clue to resolution" —Peter's confession—for as long as possible. As the confession speaks to the "faith" on which the church is built, I will deal first with the subject of Christian ethics.

Matthew's gospel carries a distinct ethical message. While that ethic is not my primary focus in this particular sermon, I do want to offer that ethic in summary form to my congregation. Concerned that the church experience healing and renewal, Matthew calls for disciples to practice forgiveness and mercy. I introduce a narrative thread consisting of ethical themes found in the Sermon on the Mount and further developed in the community discourse. I quote three Matthean pericopae that deal with love (Mt. 5:43–44), forgiveness (Mt. 18:21–22), and mercy (Mt. 5:7). Other sermons during year A of the Common Lectionary will afford preachers the opportunity to develop more fully these areas of Matthew's concern.

An ethic of love, forgiveness, and mercy is part of the foundation. This section begins by reintroducing the narrative thread of the opening parable. I refer to "a foundation of sand that will wash away in the storms of life." Anticipating what Peter will affirm in his confession, I introduce a central theme in Christian theology, incarnation. Using language found both at Matthew's beginning and ending, I speak of Jesus as God-with-us. I do not attempt to define Matthew's christology, but speak of incarnation as "the mystery of God-with-us." I am content to allow the narrative itself to affect my listeners as it will.

In this context of Matthew's christological affirmations, I finally introduce the sermon's text, Peter's confession. This section of the sermon exploits how Matthew has joined Peter's confession of Jesus as "Messiah, the Son of the living God" and Jesus' reply, "Upon this rock I will build my church." The beginning of the sermon highlighted the behavior of the foolish man and left the listener to wonder what it means to build on rock instead of sand. The narrative tension is now resolved. In Matthew's narrative, building on rock is related to our confession of Jesus as Messiah, Son of the living God, God-with-us.

And the rains will fall. I speak of the church's contemporary context and speak of controversial issues that are buffeting not only American society but the church. I do not speak to the issues themselves but to the polarizing effect they have both on church and society. The controversy over same-sex unions is current and painful for the intended audience of this sermon, a United Methodist congregation in the San Francisco Bay Area. Several congregations and pastors have recently withdrawn from the California-Nevada Annual Conference. Sixty-five pastors in the Conference are facing church trials for an act of ecclesial disobedience, participating in a service of Holy Union. The entire denomination is facing deep division and potential schism over this question. I relate this challenge to the narrative thread that has been woven through the sermon from the beginning. Rains, floods, and winds are beating against our house. I leave the congregation with a question: What are we building on?

Wise folk build houses on rock. This sermon follows an inductive logic. Up to this point the sermon has focused on the foolishness of building on sand, both literally and in the church's corporate life. I reintroduce a narrative thread from the sermon's opening moments, the wise man who built his house on rock. This section recapitulates most of the themes from the sermon, including Matthew's christological affirmations and ethical challenges. The sermon's closing moments repeat images from the opening parable (rains, floods, and winds) and from the Loma Prieta earthquake. To these images I juxtapose yet another image from the confession. Jesus promises that "the gates of Hades will not prevail" against the church he will build on rock. Thus, in its final moments, the sermon moves from a mode of challenging its listeners to reminding them of Jesus' promise. The sermon concludes with a word of grace.

5

Will It Preach?

This book began over twenty years ago with a question raised in a classroom at Princeton Theological Seminary. Literary approaches to the Bible can lead to fascinating insights into the meaning of texts. But as an M.Div. senior, about to enter the parish, I faced that perennial homiletical question: *Will it preach?* The preceding chapters represent one answer to a question that has intrigued me. I have developed a method that attempts to accomplish two purposes. First, I seek to read a sermon text in light of the entire narrative fabric of the synoptic gospel in which it is found. Second, I want to craft a sermon that exploits the narrative dynamics of that synoptic gospel.

Will it preach? That question is now squarely in your hands. I have offered one answer to the question, one way to "tell the stories of Jesus" in a way I believe is both faithful to the biblical narratives themselves and can engage congregations in the dynamics of the biblical stories. I hope this book has intrigued you, the reader, with the possibility of developing new ways "to tell the old, old story." The answer to the question—Will it preach?—cannot be found in the pages of a book. It can be developed only in the pulpits of churches across North America and around the world.

Two basic challenges face preachers who would undertake this project. First, we need to become serious readers of the Bible. Are we preachers willing to spend enough time with the text so that it engages our minds and imaginations? Second, we need to think deeply about our theology of preaching. What does it mean for us to proclaim the Word of God?

Reading the Synoptic Gospels

Robert Fulghum once made the observation, "All I really need to know I learned in kindergarten," but the sentiment does not apply to theological education.[1] Preachers often speak of all the things they *did not* learn in seminary. Beyond the practical concerns that pastors have in mind, we do not learn all we really need to know about the Bible in seminary. Hopefully, we will have acquired enough tools to continue for a lifetime the joy of reading the Bible.

My primary concern is that preachers be readers who engage biblical books. The first step in my method encourages preachers to "go on retreat" each summer with a particular synoptic gospel. I have encouraged preachers, in the course of preparing the weekly sermon, to spend considerable time researching the relationship of the sermon text with that gospel's story-as-a-whole. This research may include (but is not limited to):

- reading backward and forward in that gospel in search of narrative links;
- examining other places in that gospel where significant words, phrases, and images are also found;
- seeing the event described at a particular point in the narrative in light of the larger plot of the narrative-as-a-whole;
- exploring how the characterization of a particular figure in the text is developed.

The object of such study is to allow the preacher's mind, heart, and imagination to engage the narrative world of the text. I acknowledge that there is a significant price to pay; such research requires a significant investment of time. However, I believe this investment will pay dividends much greater than the investment of time. Weeks and years of study will lead to a deepening relationship with the narrative worlds of the Bible. It will help preachers continue

---

[1] Robert Fulghum, *All I Really Need to Know I Learned in Kindergarten: Uncommon Thoughts on Common Things* (New York: Random House, 1988).

to grow theologically and mature spiritually. It will result in biblical preaching that has immediacy and integrity.

I have a second concern related to this challenge. Many have lamented the biblical illiteracy of the people in the pews. However, I don't believe our response to the problem should be to "dumb down" our sermons so that biblically illiterate parishioners can easily understand them. One facet of the solution is to preach the stories, to tell them over and over again, until the members of our congregations know them and remember them. The other facet of the solution is to teach the Bible in small groups. Our people may have relatively little background in biblical criticism, but they *know* how to read and interpret stories. Let those discussions happen. Encourage your people to allow their imaginations to engage the biblical narratives, to dare to take the conversation beyond what they may have been "taught" the Bible means.

Toward a Theology of Preaching

What does it mean to proclaim the Word of God? Preachers answer that question in many ways. Those answers have developed out of years of biblical study, theological exploration, and pastoral experience, and I respect the deeply held points of view of my readers. My interest in the paragraphs that follow is to set forth my approach to a theology of preaching.

First, I believe that scripture—not systematic theology, not doctrine, not a particular theological tradition—is the primary focus of all Christian proclamation. When I look at the Bible (and try not to take into account what Christian theology *says* about the Bible), what do I see? I see a conversation taking place among many voices. This book has described one way of reading the conversation that continues to take place among Matthew, Mark, and Luke. Yet there are countless other voices in the Bible: from the Deuteronomistic historian to the ancient prophets of Israel, from the psalmist to the preacher of Ecclesiastes, from the poet who created Job to the storytellers who gave us Ruth and Jonah, from the evangelist John to the apostle Paul, from the writer of the pastorals and the author of James to the apocalyptic visionary who recorded Revelation.

The Bible offers entry to a conversation so rich and so deep that we can never exhaust its potential to teach, to inspire, to enrich our faith. I want to recognize and honor the conversation that is going on within the pages of scripture. I want to respond to the invitation, offered to people of faith, to participate in that conversation. I want to find creative ways, through the medium of preaching, to enable my congregation to hear and be drawn into that conversation.

Second, I want to respect the integrity of the biblical narratives-as-a-whole. To preach a sermon from a pericope apart from its context in a whole narrative is to violate the meaning of that narrative. To understand the confession of Peter without its context is not to understand it. Meaning is to be found not in an individual episode considered in isolation but in the larger narrative. In the case of the synoptic gospels, *the narrative-as-a-whole is the basic unit of meaning*.

Finally, I want to honor the biblical text as it stands without claiming an artificial theological or historical unity. Revelation takes place, in the case of the synoptics, through the medium of narrative. The reader seeking consistent records of historical events or consistent portrayals of historical figures will ultimately be frustrated. An honest reading of the three synoptic narratives reveals the existence of three competing narrative worlds with distinct plots and distinct characterizations of the characters in the stories. Revelation can take place when readers imaginatively encounter the world of each synoptic narrative. Those narratives are themselves worlds created by the word of God, worlds in which faith is formed, worlds in which wonder is awakened, worlds from which the preacher can speak, worlds into which Christian congregations are invited to come and tarry. Preaching is enriched because scripture opens up not just one but many worlds for its readers to enter. This conviction is at the heart of my hope that preachers learn to read—and congregations experience the joy of hearing—the synoptic narratives.

Selected Bibliography

Narrative Criticism and the Bible

Anderson, Janice Capel, and Stephen D. Moore, eds. *Mark & Method: New Approaches in Biblical Studies.* Minneapolis: Fortress Press, 1992. This volume contains summaries of a number of contemporary approaches to biblical criticism, including a chapter on narrative criticism written by Elizabeth Struthers Malbon.

Green, Joel B., ed. *Hearing the New Testament: Strategies for Interpretation.* Grand Rapids, Mich.: Eerdmans, and Carlisle, Cambria: Paternoster, 1995. Like Anderson and Moore's volume, this work is also a collection of articles on various approaches to biblical criticism with a chapter on narrative criticism by Mark Allan Powell.

Powell, Mark Allan. *What Is Narrative Criticism?* Minneapolis: Fortress Press, 1990. This volume offers a concise, accessible summary of the questions that narrative critics ask of a text.

Narrative Studies of the Gospel of Mark

Fowler, Robert M. *Let the Reader Understand: Reader-Response Criticism and the Gospel of Mark.* Minneapolis: Fortress Press, 1991. This work contains a cogent explanation of reader-oriented criticism. Fowler's concluding chapter offers an excellent comparison of the narrative worlds projected by the gospels of Mark and Matthew.

Juel, Donald H. *A Master of Surprise: Mark Interpreted.* Minneapolis: Fortress Press, 1994. This is a brief, accessible volume that introduces the reader to significant features of Mark's story.

Myers, Ched. *Binding the Strong Man: A Political Reading of Mark's Story of Jesus.* Maryknoll, N.Y.: Orbis Books, 1988. Myers combines a careful narrative reading of the story with a sociopolitical analysis of the world of the text.

Tolbert, Mary Ann. *Sowing the Gospel: Mark's World in Literary-Historical Perspective.* Minneapolis: Fortress Press, 1989. Tolbert offers a reading of Mark that understands the parables of the sower and the tenants in the vineyard to offer plot summaries of the two halves of the Marcan story.

Narrative Studies of the Gospel of Luke

Green, Joel B. *The Gospel of Luke.* The New International Commentary on the New Testament. Grand Rapids, Mich.: Eerdmans, 1997. This comprehensive commentary on the gospel of Luke approaches the text with a sensitivity to its narrative structure.

Johnson, Luke Timothy. *The Gospel of Luke.* Sacra Pagina 3. Collegeville, Minn.: Liturgical Press, 1991. Johnson offers another worthwhile reading of Luke's gospel.

Tannehill, Robert. *The Narrative Unity of Luke-Acts: A Literary Interpretation.* 2 Vols. Philadelphia and Minneapolis: Fortress Press, 1986 and 1990. This two-volume set represents the first extensive narrative study published on Luke-Acts.

Narrative Studies of the Gospel of Matthew

Crosby, Michael H. *House of Disciples: Church, Economics, and Justice in Matthew.* Maryknoll, N.Y.: Orbis Books, 1988. This study of Matthew's gospel is organized around the concept of "house" in the gospel. Like Myers' volume on Mark, Crosby brings his own concern for social justice to the text in an explicit way.

Kingsbury, Jack Dean. *Matthew as Story.* Philadelphia: Fortress Press, 1986. Kingsbury uses a literary-critical approach to analyze Matthew's story.

Powell, Mark Allan. *God With Us: A Pastoral Theology of Matthew's Gospel.* Minneapolis: Fortress Press, 1995. This book offers a thematic approach to Matthew's gospel, discussing mission, worship, teaching, stewardship, and social justice from a Matthean perspective.

Parable Studies in the Synoptic Gospels

Donahue, John R. *The Gospel in Parable: Metaphor, Narrative, and Theology in the Synoptic Gospels.* Philadelphia: Fortress Press, 1988. This work offers readings of Jesus' parables in their narrative context. In addition, Donahue provides a brief reading of the narrative worlds of Mark, Matthew, and Luke.

Homiletical Resources on Biblical Preaching

Holbert, John C. *Preaching Old Testament: Proclamation & Narrative in the Hebrew Bible.* Nashville: Abingdon Press, 1991. Though this volume focuses on preaching from Old Testament texts, Holbert provides a worthwhile discussion of how to use narrative categories of plot, characterization, and point of view in making the move from text to sermon.

Long, Thomas G. *Preaching and the Literary Forms of the Bible.* Philadelphia: Fortress Press, 1989. Long discusses preaching from a variety of biblical genres, including a chapter on narrative.

Wardlaw, Don M., ed. *Preaching Biblically: Creating Sermons in the Shape of Scripture.* Philadelphia: Westminster Press, 1983. This is the first volume examining the question of how to create sermons that are informed by literary approaches to biblical texts.

Homiletical Resources on the Shape of Sermons

Buttrick, David G. *Homiletic: Moves and Structures.* Philadelphia: Fortress Press, 1987. Buttrick conceives the sermon as a series of four to six "moves" organized by a conversational logic. Approaching preaching from how oral communication is perceived by listeners, his rules for structuring a "move" offer principles that can help preachers construct the sections of their sermons.

Craddock, Fred B. *Preaching.* Nashville: Abingdon Press, 1985. Craddock's work on inductive preaching is foundational for subsequent discussions of narrative and plot-shaped preaching. This work provides an excellent textbook on preaching.

Lowry, Eugene L. *The Homiletical Plot: The Sermon as Narrative Art Form.* Atlanta: John Knox Press, 1980. While sermons may not necessarily tell stories, they can be shaped in the same way that storytellers construct compelling plots. This classic work introduces the "Lowry loop."